PROFITABLE

HOTEL/MOTEL

MANAGEMENT

PROFITABLE

HOTEL/MOTEL

MANAGEMENT

William Scholz

PRENTICE HALL, INC.
Englewood Cliffs, New Jersey

Prentice-Hall International, Inc., *London*
Prentice-Hall of Australia, Pty. Ltd., *Sidney*
Prentice-Hall of Canada, Ltd., *Toronto*
Prentice-Hall of India, Private Ltd., *New Delhi*
Prentice-Hall of Japan, Inc., *Tokyo*

©1975 by

Prentice-Hall, Inc.
Englewood Cliffs, N. J.

Second Printing . . . . . October 1978

Library of Congress Cataloging in Publication Data

Scholz, William.
  Profitable hotel motel management.

  Includes index.
  1. Hotel management. 2. Motel management.
3. Food service management. I. Title.
TX911.S37   658'.91'6479473   74-32075
ISBN 0-13-728105-6

Printed in the United States of America

About the Author

William Scholz currently serves the travel industry as a consultant. In the previous decade, he was Director of Marketing and Public Relations for the American Hotel & Motel Association. This broad background has given Scholz an intimate acquaintance and knowledge of the world's finest hotels and motor inns as well as leading hoteliers here and throughout the world. The author has written numerous articles and monographs on hotel and motel operations and marketing and is the author of two popular courses offered by the Educational Institute of the American Hotel & Motel Association.

A member of the Society of American Travel Writers and Hotel Sales Management Association, Mr. Scholz is an authority on tourism promotion. He has lectured before many university and professional groups, including schools of hotel administration and travel development organizations. He is a member of the Advisory Faculty of the North American School of Travel and is the author of the Prentice-Hall book, *Communications in the Business Organization.*

FOREWORD

The aim of every business, of course, is to maximize earning potential. That's as true in the lodging industry as in publishing, real estate and dry cleaning.

One of the key problems in achieving that goal is adjusting to the rapid-fire changes within an industry. Again, that's true in the hotel field as elsewhere. And while the problem of updating and maintaining coordinated operational procedures is basically the same, obviously the courses of action within each area are different. This book presents the strategies, plans, procedures, and scientific hotel management practices to help you keep pace with—even anticipate—profitable opportunities and markets.

For years, the hotel industry was one of the most conservative fields. To John Q. Public, the industry has a basically glamorous image involving travel and constant social interaction; however, most hotel people would—perhaps begrudgingly—have to concede we moved ahead slowly in many phases of our operations.

But the years have a way of wearing down resistance and a simple, surface comparison between the hotel industry of 25 years ago with today would reflect that the industry has made greater strides since the start of the 1950s than in any other 25-year, or even half-century span of time. There isn't a single element of the lodging field that has escaped vast changes, from A to Z—architecture to the zip and zest necessary to stay abreast, if not in front of, today's trends. William Scholz has been on top of and, in many instances, instrumental in breakthroughs and innovations in the hotel/motel management field. This book is a distillation of years of first-hand knowledge and experience.

In the past quarter century, a number of new words or phrases have entered hoteliers' vocabularies such as atrium, marketing, sales "blitz," franchise, TGC and FIT, one-number reservations system, development, indoor courtyard, sauna, and female management ability. Most likely, the general manager of a property or president of a hotel company does not quarterback each idea from its conception, but he or she had better know how to guide it to termination.

Running a hotel or group of them is nothing for a gentleman farmer. Not that it ever was a lark, but today's pressures require a constant awareness of so many diverse elements that participation in a "service industry" geared to what increasingly is becoming a leisure society is not an easy feat. Maximizing that earning potential which we spoke about is no longer a case of bumping the prices on drinks in your lounge or increasing room rates. Hotel management, whether at the 20-room or 200-room or even—and perhaps most especially—at the 2,000-room level, must of necessity be concerned with ways to trim costs and expenses (or at least hold them in line) as well as knowing how much prices can be increased. That hallowed bottom line on P&L statements is a mixture of reduced overhead as well as increased revenues. Watching food or linen costs is as important as boosting room rates. This is why Mr. Scholz devotes a critical section of the book to accounting and financials.

Identifying that fine line between managing and over-managing is, at best, a difficult task. "Experience is the best teacher," someone said. You'll get no argument from me on that point, but having a well-constructed source book put together by a knowledgeable individual is the kind of educational tool that today's educators point to as a cornerstone for solid learning. This book is one of those aids. Don't just read it, use it.

Howard P. James

Chairman and President,
The Sheraton Corporation

Getting Full Value From This Book

How to increase hotel/motel revenues and reduce overhead—that's what this book is all about.

It gives practical, experience-proven solutions to management's most challenging problems. Here is a sampling of the actual big-money-generating examples in this book, the result of modern practices you can put into immediate effect in your situation:

- A 125-room hotel is saving $1,000 a year on telephone switchboard equipment alone using procedures detailed in the book. (See page 68).
- Investment of a few hundred dollars in an industry group repeatedly cited in this book saved a small motel owner $600 a month on liquor bills and more than $25,000 in construction costs.
- Savings of thousands of dollars a year on laundering are being realized by scores of hotels and motels employing the techniques the book explains. (See page 82).
- One hotel chain consistently shows profits on its food operations while many others operate restaurants at a loss. The "Secrets" of the successful food operation are revealed. (See Chapter 6).

Innkeeping professionals will find this book valuable as much for its generalist's view of hotel/motel management as for its specific suggestions in specialized functions of the business, including a wealth of bottom-line-boosting ideas and techniques not generally known or widely practiced in the industry.

This book provides step-by-step guidelines for succeeding in the innkeeping business and presents answers for the experienced innkeeper and owner helpful in planning expansion and remodeling or in analyzing present operations looking toward increased profitability.

In helping lodging industry specialists to become generalists, the intention is to impart, along with new knowledge, a far more valuable acquisition—new perceptions. These new insights should stimulate even the most experienced hotelier to re-examine and possibly reorder his priorities as well as to apply his present knowledge more effectively and rewardingly.

22 Ways This Book Will Help You Boost Profits

It tells you:

. . . how to save thousands of dollars a year on guest telephone service. See page 196.

. . . how to get the most for your money in building and modernization. See page 186.

. . . where to find hard-to-get help. See page 32.

. . . how to increase employee productivity by as much as 20 percent. See page 47.

. . . what guests want and will pay premium rates to get. See page 98.

. . . how to avoid or postpone unionization. See page 42.

. . . negotiating techniques that can prevent strikes, save thousands of dollars. See page 45.

. . . how to save money and build profits on food and beverage operations. See page 83.

. . . how to open up new markets, get more business out of old ones. See page 100.

. . . how to cash in on the international tourism boom. See page 119.

. . . how to bring in group business and fill the house on weekends. See page 125.

. . . how to avoid lawsuits. See page 163.

. . . how to design a profitable rate structure. See page 157.

. . . Conrad Hilton's nine-point success formula. See page 20.

. . . what to do about the "overbooking" problem. See page 66.

. . . how to raise capital and cut financing costs. See page 152.

. . . what to do about an "ailing" property. See page 160.

. . . what to look for in a referral or franchise affiliation. See page 130.

. . . how to avoid losses from "skippers," bad checks, "white collar thievery." See page 168.

. . . how to get your share of lucrative convention business. See page 123.

. . . how to negotiate a management contract. See page 155.

. . . guidelines for effective advertising and sales promotion. See page 102.

Highlights of Chapter One: Sophisticated management techniques that spell the difference between success and failure, Conrad Hilton's and Howard Johnson's formulas for growth and profits, trends that will revolutionize the lodging industry.

In Chapter Two: Where to find hard-to-get help, how to select new employees, the impact of OSHA, how to set up a viable compensation plan, how to postpone or avoid unionization, negotiating techniques that can prevent strikes and save thousands of dollars.

Chapter Three tells how to increase employee productivity by as much as 20 percent. It names the essentials of effective employee communication and tells how to train employees for lasting results at minimum cost.

Chapter Four covers both how to please and how to avoid displeasing guests. It spells out procedures to save time and money on "front desk" activities and suggests ways to overcome "overbooking" problems.

In Chapter Five, the unique maintenance system developed by The Sheraton Corporation is described in detail. Checklists provide money and time-saving tips on cutting water waste, reducing heating costs, trimming fuel expenditures, solving common plumbing problems, ways to slash electric bills, and how to achieve optimum maid productivity. Still another income-building idea: how to save at least 30 percent on laundry bills.

Chapter Six blueprints a pattern for food service profitability; provides tips on controlling food and food service payroll costs; covers profit-boosting portion control, imaginative menu planning and use of convenience foods; advises on how to work out a profitable restaurant leasing arrangement.

In Chapter Seven, practical answers are given on opening up lucrative, new markets and getting more business out of existing ones, how to make the most effective use of advertising budgets and media, putting the marketing approach to work to build sales.

Chapter Eight tells how to attract and service the lush and exciting international market, describes proven techniques to bring in group business and fill the house on weekends, details smart steps to avoid off-season doldrums, suggests ways to add to profits by using the services of others, tells how to improve personal selling results.

Chapter Nine deals with intelligent money management—how to bolster cash flow, techniques for controlling food and beverage costs, ways to save on payroll, how a leading budget motel chain keeps costs low, tips on record-keeping, tax savings and insurance, how to conserve and protect money.

Chapter Ten tells how to raise capital in a tight money market, how "leverage" built the Sheraton chain, points to consider in negotiating a management contract or lease, how to establish a profitable rate structure, what to do if profits are dwindling.

In Chapter Eleven, these subjects are covered: legal rights and obligations of innkeepers, how to avoid lawsuits, the innkeeper - guest relationship, new light on innkeeper's liens, what to do about "skippers" and other "deadbeats."

Chapter Twelve presents proven techniques for planning and placing effective publicity, suggests sources of news and feature stories, gives tips on radio and TV opportunities, tells how to stage a press conference, gives three rules for successful openings, blueprints award-winning programs to solve hotel/motel public relations problems and to promote profit-generating business.

Chapter Thirteen names the single most important investment an innkeeper can make, tells how occupancy and profitability can be predicted with uncanny accuracy. It lists ways to save thousands of dollars a year on guest telephone service alone. It details new construction techniques for cutting building time from months to weeks. Also covered is what guests want and will pay premium rates to get, how to use lighting effectively and how to plan facilities to attract profitable business meetings.

I urge you to put this practical book to good use. Single out a particular topic or read it through cover to cover. It represents a lifetime of experience, a storehouse of ideas, a "data band" of proven information into which you can "plug" anytime you have a firing-line challenge. Start reading and get on the highroad of new profits and personal satisfaction through the implementation of advanced hotel and motel managerial practices.

William Scholz

Acknowledgement

A debt of gratitude is acknowledged to the American Hotel & Motel Association, which the author served as Director of Marketing and Public Relations for nearly 10 years. Liberal use has been made of materials prepared by him and his associates during that period. The author has also drawn on notes compiled for his courses in hotel administration at New York University.

TABLE OF CONTENTS

1

Proven Hotel and Motel Management Techniques That Get Results

It is hard to find a complacent hotelier these days. And with good reason. Lodging industry occupancy and profits nation-wide have lagged for years. Competition is getting keener. Costs keep escalating. Competent help is difficult to attract and even harder to retain.

Small wonder that some of the deans of the industry look back wistfully on the days when a hotel manager could be reasonably successful if he wore clothes with a flair, could be constantly gracious or deferential to guests as the occasion demanded, and if he had a "following." But those days—like the 90 per cent plus occupancy rates at the end of World War II—are gone forever.

Change Challenges Lodging Industry

Today the winds of change are whistling through the lodging industry. They are causing consternation and discomfort in the executive suites of established chains and noted hotels as well as in the living quarters of the vanishing small "Mom and Pop" motels.

For, as a study sponsored by the American Hotel & Motel Association observed, the lodging industry is "an industry facing a market of tremendous potential, beset on every side by rising costs and declining service, operating in an era of truly dynamic change, that is hoping for, but not stimulating, the technological and management breakthrough to solve the problems ahead."[1]

---

[1] Operation Breakthrough (New York: American Hotel & Motel Association, 1969) p. iii.

As if that weren't enough, an incisive analysis of the lodging industry in a major business magazine reported as follows:

"The hotel and motel industry . . . a rich field that is waiting to be harvested" (by acquisition-minded corporations).

"With a few notable exceptions, lodging companies are poorly managed."

"The industry does little research into its problems, relying instead on its customers to solve many of them."

"Small, independent operators . . . If they cannot improve both their efficiency and their standards, they will be swamped."

Striking at the heart of the problem is this summation: "Some industries create and control change; others have change thrust upon them. Change in the lodging business is largely generated by relative newcomers . . . ruthlessly casting aside hallowed practices, substituting long-range planning for hasty improvisation, and investing heavily in market research, new construction techniques, and equipment."[2]

What Management Is All About

The successful hotel/motel managers of tomorrow will be those who anticipate the thrust of change, who direct or modify change, who opt for action rather than simply settle for reaction.

Success in the highly competitive, and often handsomely rewarding, field of inn-keeping requires that one progresses from the limited skills and horizons of a specialist to the broader concepts and talents of a generalist-manager. It begs the question to define managing as "getting work done through others." This is too simplistic an approach to the complex and professional skill of management. Management, far from being merely manipulative or authoritarian, is the purposive application of the techniques of planning, organizing, integrating and measuring to the business effort.

The authority of the manager—his ability to get work done through others—can stem, as pointed out by management consultant William Oncken, from competence, position, personality or character in varying mixtures or almost entirely from one or another attribute.

Management authority based on competence—acknowledged mastery of the job—is by objective measures the most desirable and effective. A manager who must rely on the organization chart to establish his authority is leading from weakness rather than strength. Those who try to get by on personality—flattery, manipulation, "being a good Joe"—seldom last long. Of all the attributes, character may well be the most essential. For competence without honesty, position without humility, personality without sincerity must all inevitably lead to failure.

---

[2]Roger Beardwood, "Reveille Sounds for the Hoteliers," *Fortune*, September 1969, pp. 110.

Authority can be conferred, as it most usually is. It can also be earned. And it can be achieved. The most rewarding authority of all though, is that which is *deserved*. It is this kind of authority, the authority of knowledge combined with character, that marks successful managers in innkeeping as in other fields.

Managing is a far more demanding task than simply being a highly paid paper shuffler or order giver. A *good* manager—and one who isn't good isn't really a manager—needs to bring to the task highly developed analytical skills to evaluate opportunities and to anticipate problems in order to establish objectives that set the appropriate priorities and that are realistic in light of the human and material resources available.

But simply pinpointing what has to be done is not enough. It is an important first step, to be sure, but the catalytic action of leadership is needed to galvanize the organization into accomplishment. And by leadership is not meant emotional haranguing or setting unachievable goals. Rather it is the approach that encourages participation and involvement because employees are helped to identify with or internalize the goals of the manager and the organization. An effective manager inspires loyalty because he is loyal to his people. He is enthusiastic and therefore his employees do the work assigned to them with enthusiasm. He is optimistic and charitable so his employees are cheerful and tolerant. In short, the effective leader motivates his people not by trickery or fear but by example and the proper combination of rewards for good performance and close supervision which makes discipline for poor performance unnecessary.

An effective manager does not tell an experienced employee *how* to do the job. Neither does he fail to give the employee adequate guidance as to what he wants done, when the job is to be completed, if and when progress reports are required, the constraints to be observed and what is to be done if unforeseen problems arise. He coordinates the work of his team, checks progress and, if necessary, reestablishes goals if the situation makes this advisable.

Finally, a good manager does not set himself apart from the goals and aspirations of his employees. He works with them to help them develop their abilities and broaden their background. He dedicates himself to creating the kind of work atmosphere that encourages and enables employees to do their best. And he recognizes that, as a manager, he is "at risk" which requires that he shoulder the responsibility and blame when things go wrong instead of passing the buck, but that he give credit and praise to his employees when things go well rather than taking the bows himself.

Hotel Managers Must Raise Sights

At a time when the need for the application of sophisticated management techniques in the innkeeping industry is urgent, faulty thinking and self-fulfilling prophecies are luxuries lodging industry managers can ill afford. The aspirant to lodging industry fame and fortune needs to understand and develop the skills to manage effectively the interrelationship of the wide variety of functions in today's hotel or motel.

Obviously, the great bulk of the future management requirements of the hotel industry must be met from college graduates of other than hotel schools, those who have taken correspondence or group study hotel training courses at the adult level, and businessmen from other fields. Already managers from conglomerates and the airlines have reached high places in the lodging industry. More will undoubtedly follow. Lodging industry leaders would do well to mark the advice to them by William Ash, once Managing Director of the 650-room International Hotel in Los Angeles: "It is my opinion that the so-called professional management would do well to realize that there are many facets of business from which they might learn."

"I don't believe that because an owner has not had previous 'hotel experience' that this precludes him from having innovative and creative ideas to bring to the hotel industry. Unfortunately, many managers feel that their expertise, gained by many years of experience, places them in a position of being above direction; when, in fact, it could very well be that their many years of experience are the same ingredients that do not allow change and/or new methods."

Howard Johnson's Operating Concepts

One of the largest organizations in the food and lodging industry is Howard Johnson's. This company's operating philosophy in serving more than 500 million customers a year revolves around five basic concepts:

1. A standard product approach embracing a standard design and a standard basis of operation in the manner of industrial organizations.
2. Limited size resulting in more efficiency, greater dispersal, better service and better control.
3. Limited service, including featuring of specialty and convenience foods.
4. "Sensible pricing"—moderate and reasonable prices and rates, based upon high volume of sales, with a low unit profit.
5. Insistence that individual units—restaurants or motels—be identified with and operated to the best interests of the communities in which they are located.

Conrad Hilton's Success Secrets

The Hilton Hotel chain bases its success on a somewhat different formula due, one would suspect, to the fact that most of its properties, including the 2,400-room Conrad Hilton Hotel in Chicago, are rather large in size. Some years ago, the founder of the chain, Conrad Hilton, named these nine secrets of his success:

1. *Turn waste space into productive use.* (An example is conversion of a storage area to a coffee shop.)
2. *Maintain the distinctive character of acquired hotels.* (New York's Plaza, once a Hilton property, has retained its traditional ambiance through a succession of managements.)
3. *Stress efficiency, but not standardization.* (The popular joke about waking up in a Hilton Hotel and not being able to tell which city or country one was in, is more a tribute to that chain's attention to guest convenience than an indictment of the sameness of exterior appearance or decor.)

4. *Consolidate facilities.* (Linen supplies stored next to the laundry operation and repair room illustrates one application.)
5. *Achieve income from store rentals.* (Hilton pioneered in converting extra space in cavernous hotel lobbies into income-producing and guest-pleasing shops.)
6. *Emphasize guest service.* (The expression, "the customer is always right," might well have originated in the hospitality industry. The "Lady Hilton" service offering specially designed rooms and amenities for female guests exemplifies this concept.)
7. *Keep in personal touch with operations.* (The most commonly heard criticism of the management of many large hotels is that it exists in an ivory tower divorced from the problems—and the satisfactions—of day-to-day operations.)
8. *Diversify.* (Individuals with the financial resources of a Conrad Hilton are few and far between, but the advice concerning not keeping all your eggs in one basket applies across the board. Often the profits from a coffee shop or small bar can mean the difference between success and failure for a small operation. Larger ones can diversify by catering at a nearby ski resort or airport or, if the business is a seasonal one, by acquiring a property in a different climate. Chains are pushing diversification even further by acquiring travel agencies, bus lines and hotel supply firms, as well as campgrounds and other businesses.)
9. *Apply modern industrial methods to hotel operations.* (This counsel, of course, was what lay behind AH&MA's decision to sponsor "Operation Breakthrough," the first really comprehensive and objective study ever undertaken of the American lodging industry from a systems point of view. A whole array of management and operating techniques developed by the American manufacturing industry can be applied rewardingly to lodging industry operations.)

Trends That Will Affect Innkeepers

Undoubtedly the most important single requirement for success in the innkeeping business in the years ahead is the ability to recognize, anticipate, and adapt to change. A number of trends that have emerged in recent years are expected to continue and even accelerate in the late Seventies.

- Chains will account for an ever-increasing share of the market. Today they own, franchise or represent about a third of all the nation's hotels and motels. R. L. Kirkpatrick, former President and Chairman of the Board, the Downtowner Corporation, says "Survival of the small company in the food and lodging business today is impossible . . . to grow in this field, any corporation must become a full-service organization."
- New life styles and emerging new markets will result in increased demands for Spartan or budget-type accommodations with a concomitant reduction in services such as room service, and even a willingness on the part of the guest to perform some services for himself such as bedmaking, in return for a lower rate. Group travelers, visitors from abroad, minority groups, young people and senior citizens will make up these markets.

- Due to changes in modes of travel and the high cost of downtown real estate, motor hotels and airport hotels will proliferate while many center city properties will wither on the vine.
- High labor costs and the problem of poor weekend occupancy could lead a number of hotels to adopt a six or five-day week with the property being closed on Saturdays and/or Sundays.
- There will be considerable growth in resort-convention complexes and facilities especially designed for business meetings of which, it has been estimated, there are more than 300,000 a year.
- Travel facilitating services will grow and improve. Credit card use in hotels will expand as will methods of rapidly checking the credit standing of card holders. Registration and check-out will be speeded and simplified through the use of electronic data processing. Instant reservation services will not only book a hotel room but also reserve a car, an airplane seat, and "two on the aisle" for a Broadway show in keeping with the trend toward packaging the total travel experience.

Predictions for the Future

Among developments and trends predicted for the years ahead by lodging industry leaders are these:

—Within the next 10 years, giant airport megastructures will merge all transportation, hotel and business facilities under one roof, with total reservation systems providing one-stop travel shopping.

—The idea of a space hotel is not as far-fetched as it might seem. Nine companies have already submitted bids in the United States for the development of a shuttle service between space stations and earth.

—A 10% increase in available rooms world-wide is forecast for the next few years. Holiday Inns has a goal of 3,000 motels by 1980. Ramada plans 1,000 properties in 5 years. Sheraton, Loews, Western International, Hilton and Hyatt Corporation all plan as many as 100 new properties each in the United States and overseas in the next few years. Intercontinental Hotels is planning a chain of 1,000 room hotels geared to the requirements of economy travelers.

—Baggage handling problems could turn out to be merely academic in the future. One American company is planning a service where airplane passengers will simply drive their cars on the plane, keeping the luggage in the car. Parking their cars on a lower level, passengers will take seats on the upper level for the flight. On arrival at destination the passengers will simply get in their cars, drive down a ramp and off to their destination. Each of the planes that will be used is planned to accommodate 46 cars carrying four persons in each car.

—The hotel of tomorrow may be made up of "instant" rooms—modular units that can be moved to accommodate changing needs. Additional rooms could be added to an operation during peak periods and removed during slack times thereby decreasing maintenance. Even remodeling and redecorating could be simplified by merely slipping out the room on which work had to be done and replacing it temporarily with a substitute unit.

—A number of companies are already in the process of designing a lunar hotel. Some of the plans contemplate building under the moon's surface for radiation protection and to insure a constant temperature. An outside view would be achieved via large, wall-mounted, closed-circuit colored television screens. Rooms would be entered by an airlock. Glass and equipment cleansing in bars and restaurants would be accomplished by laser beams. Ramada Inns has planned a lunar hotel which would consist of a series of inflatable spheres set on telescopic legs, joined by flexible tubular corridors. For venturing outdoors, guests would be provided with space suits pressurized with an oxygen supply.

—Students at Cornell University have planned a modified, semi-submerged *underwater* hotel which would be located in the United States Virgin Islands and which they estimate could be completed and in operation in a few years.

Not 30 years away, but predicted for the next 10 years are these types of equipment:

- A refrigerator without a door, but employing an air screen to keep the cold in and the warm air out.
- Self-cleaning equipment—ovens and fryers that will drain and clean themselves at the push of a button.
- Disappearing dishes, pots and pans that will eliminate the problem of cleaning tableware. The dishes will be chemically constructed to dissolve at a certain temperature.
- A power-pack unit that will use garbage as a source of light and power and provide a method of getting rid of the garbage as well.

Designers are said to be considering ideas such as these for possible future implementation: Climate-controlled domes using solar energy; computerized lighting allowing continuous changing light so that no 24 hour period is the same; programmed color lights to change decorative design; restaurants without walls where tables are constructed of different materials so each patron can seek out the setting that suits his mood; taped sounds to simulate rainfall, the surf and woodland noises.

Additional innovations under consideration are self-regulating window glass, airflow doors and walls, automated room service, outdoor air conditioning, luminescent walls, bi-metallic heating and cooling, and automatic bedmaking.

Five Major Problem Areas for Hotel/Motel Managers

Challenging as the future changes in the areas of technology and marketing may be, the greatest challenge of all will be in the field of management. Five major problem areas have been identified which will trouble industrial managers and innkeepers as well:

1. *Managerial leadership shortage*—not of people to fill jobs, but the availability of individuals with the requisite competency and capacity for growth.
2. *Impact of Automation and Computerization*—on decision-making, long-range planning, organizational structure, and motivation of employees.
3. *New approaches to organization and management*—temporary "task force" groupings bringing together highly skilled specialists and requiring a more supportive managerial style with more attention being paid to relationships than structure.
4. *Internationalization*—the growth of multi-national businesses and the limitations imposed by size, the need for such companies to develop the product mix, market techniques and technology to keep competitive in a world-wide market economy.
5. *Societal problems*—urbanization, mass transit, low-cost housing, environmental control, the poor and the aged, unemployed, handicapped, minorities, and education.

Management by Objectives

One highly effective tool for meeting the challenges facing today's managers is Management by Objectives. A systematic, disciplined approach to objectives, using methods of analysis and measurement, MBO basically is a process of making and keeping promises. Periodically the manager and those reporting to him agree on their objectives and commit themselves to achieving them. MBO has been described as a system of management that relates long-run plans and short-term goals and which is totally results-oriented.

Management by Objectives is utilized to some degree by most major hotel/motel chains. Braniff Hotels, for example, sets up par budgets and holds management accountable for performance related to budget. At Sonesta International and Inter-Continental Hotels, management incentive plans are based on attainment of goals mutually agreed upon by the manager and his superior.

At one location, the goals agreed upon by the manager and his food and beverage manager included:

1. Reduce food costs to 40 percent of sales.
2. Cut labor cost to below 32 percent.
3. Increase group business by at least 10 percent over previous year.
4. Increase cocktail lounge sales by 15 percent.
5. Maintain employee turnover at less than 10 percent.
6. Develop an assistant capable of replacing food and beverage manager within a year.
7. Prepare a procedures manual for food and beverage department.

Among the uses of MBO in a hotel/motel enterprise are these:

Performance appraisal	Self-management
Planning	Salary administration
Coaching and Counseling	Incentive plan rewards
Self-development	Manpower planning

Following are five necessary elements in a successful MBO program:

1. Long-range planning
2. Clearly defined and attainable objectives
3. Commitment to specific results
4. Provision for periodic feedback
5. Measurable goals

Managing by Results

A somewhat similar approach is that called "Managing by Results." This is an approach that calls for the setting of higher but realistic profit objectives and then lining up every function of the business to support the profit target and to permit it to be realized. Principles of Management by Results include:

1. Top management must establish the major objectives for the enterprise. These furnish direction to all employees and facilitate delegation as well.
2. The responsibility for results must be delegated. The results of all delegated responsibilities must add up to the total profit objective sought.
3. Each manager in the enterprise should be assigned definite profit improvement objectives, not only to give direction to his work, but to aid in the measurement of his performance.

Leadership Style Influences Morale, Performance

There is a definite and relatively consistent relationship between the leadership style and management system of an organization and the extent to which it is able to achieve its objectives, the Institute for Social Research of the University of Michigan has found. Its long-time director writes that the kind of organization developed by the most successful managers is:

A human system made up of interlocking work groups with a high degree of group loyalty among members and favorable attitudes and trust between supervisors and subordinates. Sensitivity to others and relatively high levels of skill in personal interaction and the functioning of groups also are present. These skills permit effective participation in decisions on common problems. Participation is used, for example, to establish organizational objectives which are a satisfactory integration of the needs and desires of all members of the organization and of persons functionally related to it. High levels of reciprocal influence occur, and high levels of total coordinated influence are achieved in the organization. Responsibility for the organization's success is felt individually by the members and each initiates action, when necessary, to assure that the organization accomplishes its objectives. Communication is efficient and effective. There is a flow from one part of the organization to another of all relevant information important for each decision and action. The leadership in the organization has developed what might well be called a highly effective social system for interaction and mutual influence.[3]

Tools and Techniques for Better Management

A number of sophisticated management tools and techniques hold promise of rewarding application in the lodging industry. Probably the most basic is systems analysis. This technique is a circular process, a cycle of (1) defining objectives, (2) designing alternative systems to achieve those objectives, (3) evaluating the alternatives in terms of their effectiveness and costs, (4) questioning the objectives and other assumptions underlying the analysis, (5) opening up new alternatives, (6) establishing new objectives, and then repeating the whole process through new cycles.

Obviously management information systems made possible by advanced computers will benefit from improved data acquisition, data processing, data analysis, data retrieval and data reporting. Through computer service bureaus, even small hotels and motels can take advantage of computerization. For a fee, such an organization makes available its computers (the "hardware") and the programming (the "software") to effectively serve its customers. The computer can not only convert raw data into information to help run a business more effectively, but it also has the capability of printing out payroll checks, mailing labels—even personalized letters. In the lodging industry, in addition to these applications, computers are being used successfully in reservations systems, room management, accounting, sales and marketing, food and beverage control and forecasting.

Forecasting, or "futuristics" as it is sometimes called, is a fundamental part of modern business planning. Its purpose is to equip managers to make better choices. It involves:

A. An examination of possible events and the probabilities of their taking place;
B. An assessment of the interactions among these events;
C. Identification of those events that can be controlled and the extent to which such control is possible;
D. Evaluation of alternative future possibilities considering to what degree they might be controlled, and;
E. Finally, arriving at an assessment of the impact of the possible future.

---

[3]Rensis Likert, "*Human Organizational Measurements:* Key to Financial Success," *Michigan Business Review*, May, 1971, p. 2.

Using a model of its property programmed into a computer, the Disneyland Hotel in California is able to forecast profit and loss, cash flow and balance sheet statements for as far as five years into the future. The generation of a five year detailed profit and loss projection takes only 45 minutes.

PERT is Pertinent

Another valuable management tool useful in reducing costs and improving planning and control is Program Evaluation Review Technique. Known as PERT, it is a method that identifies when, where and by whom decisions are made. The PERT technique is based on a graphic representation (the PERT network) of the steps necessary to complete a particular job as well as the operations that connect the various steps. The steps, or "events," are points in time marking the beginning or completion of specific tasks in the assignment while the operations, or "activities," are the mental or physical processes connecting one "event" with another. Utilizing this information, the manager can foretell the consequences of variations from a logical plan and, more important, take remedial steps *before* the deviation takes place.

In showing graphically how certain tasks in a given job must be completed before others can be initiated, PERT identifies the key activities related to the main function (the critical path) and also pinpoints auxiliary activities which are required and may be performed concurrently. At the same time, it highlights the slack/float, delay and lost time involving employees waiting for a critical activity to be completed.

In its most basic form, PERT is exemplified by the familiar bar chart used to keep track of construction progress. Sonesta, for example, employed this technique widely in the construction, staffing and operation of its European properties. Inter-Continental Hotels uses it to prepare staffing tables so the required people and skills are available as needed at various phases of construction and operation of a new property. Progress charts are also helpful in planning for delivery and installation of furniture, fixtures and equipment.

Flow charting has been introduced into the industry by consulting firms and has been helpful in identifying the "critical path" of operations and procedures.

PERT, however, has been less widely used in improving operating efficiency and employee productivity, areas where it is capable of making substantial contributions.

In one large resort hotel complex, the number of daily charges originating from various points of sale to be posted to individual guest accounts was giving the night staff fits.

A PERT network was diagrammed to show the various activities performed in the night audit procedure, the sequence of "events" representing the beginning or end of each activity and the time required to perform each activitiy. With the aid of the diagram, it was possible to identify the key activities relating to the main function (the critical path), auxiliary activities and slack-float or delay time.

Auxiliary activities are those that are done concurrently with the critical activities while slack-float or delay time represents time lost by employees while waiting for a critical activity to be completed.

In analyzing the PERT network, the object is to eliminate delays and to set up the most expeditious way of accomplishing the critical activities.

By reassigning duties and balancing job functions after study of the PERT network, management of the resort hotel complex was able to achieve a considerable reduction in slack-float time and a more efficient night auditing operation with fewer employees required.

Summing Up: PERT can point the way to more productive personnel, simplified procedures and faster, more efficient, operations as well as reduced costs. It can be applied in accounting, scheduling of housekeeping and maintenance, room reservations, laundry and kitchen production scheduling and many other activities where time and cost relationships are important.

12 Management Tools for Future Success

1. *Electronic Data Processing:* Compiling, sorting, processing and reporting information using electronic hardware and software.

2. *Management Information Systems:* Any specially designed method (manual or computer based) to provide management with needed information on a regular basis.

3. *Management by Objective:* Establishing specific objectives for the company, for each of its major functions or departments and, usually, for key individuals with accountable individuals helping to set their goals.

4. *Organizational Development:* Study of the organization, particularly its human resources, aimed at finding present and future weaknesses and taking steps to effect necessary improvements.

5. *Direct Costing-Marginal Costing:* Method of apportioning costs between fixed and variable and for identifying costs as being directly associated with and affected by the volume of individual profit centers.

6. *Discounted Cash Flow Analysis:* Examination of projected revenues and/or expenses over a period of years resulting from a given investment or decision and discounting them at a given rate (usually cost of capital) to determine their "present value" as a basis for facilitating comparison of various alternatives.

7. *Systems Approach:* Viewing an organization as an integrated complex of interdependent parts inter-reacting among themselves and with their environment. Systems engineering applies this concept to planning and control of physical processes.

8. *Job Enrichment:* Changing the nature or structure of jobs to make them more meaningful. Involves giving employees more responsibility for planning and evaluating their own work and providing them with greater opportunity for participation in decision making.

9. *Indirect Work Measurement:* Measuring the work volume and content of *nonproduction* jobs to arrive at efficient staffing levels and to control productivity costs.

10. *Modeling:* Simulating conditions in order to predict or control. Modeling usually, but not always, involves mathematics and electronic data processing.

11. *Operations Research:* The variety of mathematical techniques used to apply an analytical approach to a business problem.

12. *Social Accounting:* Assignment of monetary values to non-economic consequences of decisions (effects on ecology, race relations, company reputation). Factoring these values in with profit and loss analysis in arriving at investment decisions and/or in appraising executive performance.

2

Staffing for
Increased Productivity
in Hotels and Motels

There are at least two good reasons why every innkeeper can profit from paying greater attention to his employees. One is that, since the lodging industry seems to offer relatively limited opportunities for the application of improved technology—to say nothing of automation—and costs seem destined to keep going ever higher, improved productivity and performance on the part of employees may represent the best chance for realizing operating savings and improving profits.

The other is that, in a service business such as innkeeping, especially when this is becoming increasingly dominated by chain operations, convenience food and standardized operating techniques, the ounce of difference that can mean success for some properties while others fail has got to be the ability, training, dedication, involvement, interest and service orientation of employees.

With management dependent on employees for the most important ingredient of success in the hotel business—guest satisfaction—and payroll and related expenses accounting for approximately one third of the distribution of the income dollar, the money and effort expended in obtaining, training and retaining qualified and highly motivated personnel can easily be among the most rewarding investments a manager can make.

Personnel Includes Many Activities

The personnel function embraces a wide spectrum of activities. It begins with a thinking through of employee relations *policies*—considerations of leadership style, relationships, responsibilities, philosophy, societal orientation and organizational structure. In all except the smallest organizations, policies should be put into writing and distributed to key people to provide guidance and insure consistent application. Policies, of course, should be reviewed periodically in light of changing conditions.

Personnel concerns itself with each of these broad areas:

A. *Employment*—Recruiting, interviewing, psychological and aptitude testing, selection and medical exams. Along with this goes administration of transfers, promotions and terminations as well as responsibility for adherence to anti-discrimination laws.

B. *Education and Training*—Orientation of new employees, educational aid for employees, training of both employees and supervisors, executive development and communication.

C. *Health and Safety*—Occupational health, emergency medical care, safety program, preventive medicine.

D. *Employee Services*—Cafeteria, vending machines, employee lounge, lockers, counseling, suggestion system.

E. *Wage and Salary Administration*—Salary structure, performance standards and job evaluation, salary surveys.

F. *Benefits*—Group insurance, sick pay plan, hospitalization, major medical coverage, key man insurance, pension plan, social security.

G. *Labor Relations*—Representation elections, collective bargaining, grievance procedures.

H. *Administration*—Personnel records, turnover statistics, security, holidays and vacations, office layout and services, work rules.

How to Obtain Good Employees

Although hiring is frequently done unwisely, without adequate reference to the organization chart, manning table or job analysis, these tools are vital elements in employment planning. The organization chart indicates both overall job responsibilities and relationships as well as specifying the "pecking order" within the organization. The chief value of the manning table is to indicate lines of promotion or possible transfer and to "red flag" incipient employment problems such as dead end jobs, absence of qualified successors for key positions, overstaffing in certain functions or a work force heavily weighted with older employees.

All too often in hiring, there is an inadequate understanding of what the job consists of and what qualities the candidate should possess. The key to successful hiring is *job analysis* which spells out in writing every aspect, duty and responsibility of the job to be filled. Job analysis involves observing the job, interviewing the employee performing it and writing down what is learned. It leads to writing of a *job description* which tells what the job is and how it is performed and a *job specification* listing the skills and qualities necessary to perform the job. Forms for use in conducting a job analysis are available from your State Employment Service. Often, as a by-product of job analysis, inefficiencies are revealed which can, if corrected, result in better performance by employees and sizable cost savings.

Filling a vacant position shouldn't necessarily mean always going outside the organization. While it is desirable for organizational vitality and growth to seek an infusion of "new blood" from time to time, consideration also needs to be given to the qualifications and aspirations of employees already on the payroll. Very often the known quantity with understanding of the company "ropes" is a far better choice for upgrading to a vacancy than a new hire who might be overqualified or have problems in relating to the new situation.

If it is determined to go outside, however, there are a number of sources of employees other than the obvious newspaper, trade press, and radio advertising, employment agencies, the State Employment Service and direct recruitment at schools and colleges. Among these additional sources: temporary help agencies, neighborhood and "shopper" publication ads, friends of employees, suppliers and nearby firms, clergymen, vocational rehabilitation centers, various organizations to aid the handicapped, welfare agencies, court probation officers, fraternal and social groups, and retired military personnel.

Schools offering correspondence courses in hotel/motel management, as well as the Educational Institute of AH&MA, maintain lists of qualified graduates and are anxious to cooperate in placing them.

In many areas "Project Transition," a Department of Defense program to help servicemen prepare for civilian jobs while they are still in the service, can provide trained innkeeping help.

Secondary schools can be a prime source of talent for the lodging industry. Every hotel/motel manager can help improve the industry's image in terms of career opportunities—and assure himself of a valuable local labor pool at the same time—by doing these things:

- Become visible in the community as a knowledgeable, involved and successful businessman
- Work with local educators to have hospitality education courses included in school curricula
- Cooperate with school guidance counselors in making available information on lodging industry careers to students
- Offer part-time and summer employment to interested young people
- Develop promotions which will attract young people to your property
- Offer free meeting space for worthwhile student activities or projects
- Take advantage of opportunities to speak about the lodging industry and careers it offers at schools and before church groups, civic clubs, etc.
- Sponsor open house or tours of your property for faculty and students as well as appropriate civic groups

The real secret of effective recruiting is continuity. Rather than only becoming active when there are jobs to be filled, skilled personnel people anticipate vacancies and interview potential employees regularly in order to maintain a file of qualified and screened people against the time they might be needed.

Tips on Conducting Interviews

In interviewing an applicant, the purposes are to learn whether he has the skills, experience and motivation the job requires and to give a good picture of the job, the organization, and the rewards. It is essential that this be a two-way sharing of information rather than an inquisition. In addition to having on hand a description of the job to be filled and the job specifications, as well as a copy of the applicant's resumé or application blank, the interviewer should have full and accurate information about pay, overtime, promotional opportunities, and company policies which might be of concern to the applicant.

The interview should be conducted in privacy, at a leisurely pace and free from interruptions. Of all the suggestions that could be made on the conduct of the interview, the one most important is *"Be Yourself."* Particularly if the new employee is to work for the person doing the interviewing, aside from the exchange of factual information, the interview should reveal whether the "chemistry" of the relationship would be right.

Surprisingly, not all organizations check an applicant's references. If they do, they frequently settle for a form letter which encourages a form reply and which usually tells little or nothing helpful about the subject. Reference checks are best conducted by telephone since this provides the opportunity to form judgements based on factors such as hesitancy in answering pointed questions and nuances in replies.

While there are those who have reservations about psychological testing, it can be very useful in helping to select key management people since it often brings out problems of motivation, attitudes or relationships which might not be revealed in the personal interview. As a caveat, though, it must be mentioned that psychological testing has limitations and selection primarily on the basis of the findings of such tests would generally prove unsatisfactory.

Aptitude testing, like the psychological tests, can prove useful in the selection process, but is probably superfluous for high skill jobs and not worthwhile for low skill ones. The best test overall is the pragmatic one of job performance. Wherever feasible, an applicant—such as a typist or pastry chef—should be asked to demonstrate his ability rather than just tell about it. In all testing an employer must be careful not to run afoul of the U.S. Equal Employment Opportunity Commission. The only safe course is to give only those tests that measure skills essential to the work.

In view of the effect of health on attendance and job performance as well as group insurance and salary continuance costs, it is remarkable that many otherwise prudent organizations do not require a medical examination prior to employment. Such a simple and relatively inexpensive precaution should be taken not only with food handling personnel but all employees, particularly those who will occupy key management positions.

Welcoming the New Employee

When the new employee reports for work, the first order of business should be a sincere personal welcome by the person to whom he will be reporting. He should be given an employee handbook, if the organization has one, told about the organization, how his job fits in, the standards of performance which will be expected, and all he needs to know about such things as working hours, payday, lunch periods, safety rules, holidays and the benefits package available to him. As soon as it is convenient, he should be introduced to his co-workers.

Most important, the new employee should be told at the outset about his relationship with others in the organization at the same or higher levels and his responsibilities; authority and accountability should be very clearly and specifically delineated. It is a sad commentary on many orientation plans that the new employee is often filled in thoroughly on company history the first day on the job, but is forced to stub his toe time and time again before the parameters of his job are established.

Implementing An Effective Training Program

Unfortunately, a great many employees in the lodging industry are neither well educated nor highly motivated. This complicates the training problem since the incentive to learn new skills that don't promise an immediate pay-off is low and resistance to new ways of doing things is often high.

Some hotel/motel operators feel that money spent on training is wasted because the typically nomadic employee will only move on to another job elsewhere in a matter of time. Yet there is persuasive evidence that, even if this is so, money spent on a well planned training program for employees is an investment that pays prompt and tangible dividends. It has been estimated that training can increase employee efficiency by as much as 25 percent. Among the benefits of a training program for employees are these: improved performance; reduction in accidents, waste and spoilage, absenteeism and turnover; and increased production.

Training should take place under the following conditions:

    a. when new employees are hired.
    b. when employees are given jobs demanding new skills or procedures.
    c. when duties, organization or relationships change.

In addition to on-the-job and "vestibule" training of employees, a variety of other training techniques are available. Training films and film strips are effective and programmed learning, in which the individual sets his own pace, is particularly appropriate for slow learners or those with a language problem.

Supervisory training and executive development programs may make use of short courses at schools of hotel administration, seminars conducted by groups such as the American Management Association or industry associations like the American Hotel & Motel Association and the Hotel Sales Management Association. Of particular value to properties not having a formal supervisory or executive development program of their own is the Career Development Program of AH&MA's Educational Institute which makes available more than 25 authoritative courses on every phase of hotel/motel management and which may be studied with a group or by correspondence.

Communication Makes the Wheels Go 'Round

Administrative communication is that interchange of interest, unity of purpose and unity of effort in a group of individuals organized to achieve a specific mission. An effective communication activity in a hotel or motel should, as a minimum, (1) assist in the attainment of the operating objectives of the business, (2) help improve performance and job satisfaction of employees at all levels, and (3) keep management informed of attitudes and reactions among employees as an aid to decision-making and control. Suggestions on rewarding communication techniques will be made in the next chapter.

Impact of OSHA on Employers

Concern for employee health and safety is so deeply ingrained in management today that little need be said about this area except that the growing menace of drug use poses a new and serious threat to employee welfare and operating efficiency as well as to guest satisfaction and security. Annual physicals for all employees paid for by management can alert employees to incipient serious illness in time to initiate preventive treatment. Of course, results of physicals should be known only to the physician and the employee.

Under the Federal Occupational Safety and Health Act of 1970, an employer must maintain a log of occupational injuries and illnesses as well as a supplementary record of each. A summary must be posted at the end of each calendar year. Employees must be informed of the provisions of the Act. Each workplace accident or health hazard resulting in one or more fatalities or the hospitalization of five or more employees must be reported to the Secretary of Labor within 48 hours.

Employers' responsibilities for providing a safe work environment were increased considerably as a result of the passage of the Occupational Safety and Health Act, which became effective April 28, 1971.

Employer duties spelled out broadly in the Act:

1. ". . .to furnish to each employee employment and a place of employment free from recognized hazards that are causing or likely to cause death or serious physical harm. . ."
2. Compliance ". . . with the Occupational Safety and Health Standards and all rules pursuant to the Act except where an approved state plan is in effect."

Highlights of the Act include the following:

- Premises can be inspected at any reasonable time without delay by an OSHA Compliance Officer to see if your establishment does conform to the required safety and health standards. Also, your establishment will normally be inspected by an OSHA Compliance Officer whenever there is a fatality, or if five or more employees are hospitalized as the result of one incident in your establishment. All pertinent conditions, structures, machines, apparatus, the devices and materials therein can be checked. Except in rare instances, you will have no advance notice that your business is going to be visited by OSHA.

- Any employee (or representative thereof) who believes you are in violation of a job safety or health standard, or believes that an imminent danger exists, may request an inspection by OSHA. If OSHA believes the complaint is valid, they may inspect not only the alleged violation but your entire establishment for other violations of safety or health standards.

- Where violations are noted, they will be discussed with you. You will be issued a written citation describing the specific nature of the apparent violation and be given a reasonable time for abatement of the alleged violation.

- Citations issued for serious violations incur a penalty up to $1,000.00 for each violation, while optional penalties up to the same amount may be incurred for non-serious violations where cited. Penalties of up to $10,000 for each violation can be incurred for willful or repeated violations of employer duties. In some cases, the employer can be imprisoned for willful violations.

- You may be required to keep records on work-related injuries or illnesses. You must keep required records on work-related deaths, or where there is multiple hospitalization of 5 or more employees as the result of an employment accident.

- You are required to have the OSHA posting notice, "Safety and Health Protection on the Job," permanently posted in a conspicuous location in your establishment.

- If a Compliance Officer feels that there is imminent danger to employees, that normally could be expected to cause death or serious physical harm before the danger could be eliminated through normal channels, he can ask that the affected operation(s) be shut down. If need be, a court order can be obtained.

The law provides for financial assistance to small firms in order to comply with the standards if the Small Business Administration determines that the firm is likely to suffer substantial economic injury without such assistance. For additional information, a fact sheet entitled "Fact Sheet For Small Businesses On Obtaining Compliance Loans"—OSHA Form 2005—is available from the nearest office of OSHA.

Important Safety Precautions

Safety and fire prevention measures should be taken to protect both employees and guests. It is estimated that more than 12,000 fires take place in hotels and motels each year and nearly 1,000 lives have been lost in such fires over the past 100 years. A great many of these lives could have been saved by the observance of one cardinal rule: In case of fire notify guests immediately and don't delay in calling the fire department.

The best source of information and materials on accident and fire prevention is the National Safety Council, 425 North Michigan Avenue, Chicago, Illinois 60611. Excellent suggestions on special fire precautions where handicapped people are involved are available from the American Hotel & Motel Association, 888 Seventh Ave., N.Y., N.Y. 10019.

Preventing loss of life, limb, time, and property as a result of accidents calls for a diligently applied program of safety planning and training. It should include steps to accomplish the following:

1. Accident prevention.
2. Determining the cause of accidents that occur.
3. Minimizing the chances of repetition.
4. Establishing procedures for speedy and efficient handling of emergencies.
5. Involving every member of supervision and the staff in accident prevention.

Bulletin board notices, as well as written and oral communication to employees, should call particular attention to the following common safety hazards:

1. Leaving rolled up rugs, carpets, or similar objects in rooms or hallways where they create a tripping hazard.
2. Unsecured rugs or mats, or slick unpolished floors in any area.
3. Permitting food or drinks to be carelessly spilled on floors, creating a slipping hazard.
4. Allowing foreign objects to find their way into food and drink.
5. Permitting the following dangerous or defective equipment in guest or public rooms: Frayed or improperly insulated electric fixtures, broken glassware with sharp edges, broken faucet handles, woodwork with splinters, locks that will not operate smoothly or at all, faulty hot water mixing valves in the bathroom, protruding nails or tacks, inadequately supported mirrors, pictures, or other objects hanging from the walls or ceiling.
6. Creating slipping hazards through careless mopping and polishing of floor areas.
7. Overcrowding and shoving in elevators, closing doors or moving the car while passengers are entering or leaving, and mishandling of luggage in cars.
8. Permitting revolving doors with obvious defects to remain operative.
9. Unsafe handling of knives, glassware, razor blades, or other sharp objects.
10. Lack of care in use of carpenter and plumbing equipment, meat cutters, cleavers, saws, and meat grinders.
11. Use of such things as chairs, boxes and books as supports instead of ladders to reach elevated objects.
12. Attempts to lift or move heavy objects, beyond the capacity of one person, or failure to observe accepted safe lifting practices.
13. Attempts at self-treatment for cuts and injuries.

Wage and Salary Administration

Man may not live by bread alone, but the "bread" he earns is a mighty important consideration to him. Setting up a viable salary structure and devising a system to insure compensation appropriate to the employee's contributions to the success of the enterprise are among the most challenging tasks management must face. Good management practice suggests that they should begin with a system of formal job evaluation to establish the relative worth of various jobs within the organization.

In making the evaluations, consideration needs to be given to factors such as physical effort, education, experience and skill required, working conditions, responsibilities, and effect of decisions on the business.

The next step, having established relationships among the jobs in the hotel/motel, is to set up a wage scale-salary structure. What is paid in the community for comparable work will largely determine what pay for particular jobs should be, but factored in should be anticipated tip income and the value of meals and lodging provided certain employees.

The structure should establish pay ranges for each position so an employee may see the possibility of future financial reward based on improved performance in his present job while at the same time being reminded that "the sky is not the limit" for pay unless he moves into a more demanding job or he has a significant change in duties and responsibilities. Levels in the structure should provide for a salary range overlap so an employee performing exceptionally well at one level may earn more than one doing only an adequate job in a position rated at the next higher level.

Not a few companies take the easy way out in wage and salary administration by resorting to periodic so-called "merit" increases which are really only automatic sweeteners paying tribute to seniority. Far too often such increases are rewards for inefficiency. It makes a great deal more sense to revise the whole salary structure upward periodically in these inflationary times so the top pay possible for each level is increased, but performance rather than seniority should be the criterion used in determining how often and by how much pay should be increased. In all salary decisions, the best guideline is *pay for performance*.

Evaluating Performance

Employee performance rating, which should take place at regular intervals—usually annually in connection with salary reviews—deserves attention for several reasons. First, objective rating of job performance forms the basis for decisions on pay increases. Second, the vast majority of employees want a periodic and scheduled opportunity to learn how they are doing and to discuss job problems with their supervisor or manager. Finally, the performance evaluation discussion enables the "boss" to explore paths of future progress with the employee and what steps the employee should take to improve his value to the organization.

The important thing to remember about employee rating—whether it is done by check list, ranking of employees in the work group or on a scale of values—is that its ultimate purpose is to develop better personal relationships and to improve performance. With this in mind, these suggestions from an earlier book by the author might prove helpful.[1]

What you should try to accomplish:	*. . . so the employee can:*
1. Build a better working relationship by getting to know the man better, by letting him know you respect him and are sincerely interested in his progress and his opinions.	1. Express his opinions freely, tell you his personal problems and aspirations, the reasons for his actions. Get help in solving any special problems he has encountered on the job.
2. Let the man know what is expected of him. Review the position guide	2. Benefit by a realistic reappraisal, if necessary, of the job requirements,

[1]William Scholz, *Communication in the Business Organization* (Englewood Cliffs, N. J.; Prentice-Hall, Inc., 1962) p. 140.

and the standards (accountability factors) by which he is measured. Tell him of your personal preferences about the way he performs the job.

the importance of his contribution, etc..

3. Give the man recognition and praise for good performance or abilities. This will build up his self-confidence and make him want to do still better.

3. Make more effective use of his special abilities and be encouraged to suggest improvements in the job.

4. Point out tactfully those areas in which his performance falls short of the job requirements or your expectations.

4. Tell you the reasons why it is difficult or impossible to do the job as you want it done.

5. Explain salary and other administrative matters as they affect the employee and his job.

5. Discuss and reach a clearer understanding of what he might expect in terms of salary and promotion on his present job. Overcome misunderstanding and confusion about authority and responsibility.

6. Work with him in developing a program for his self-improvement for future progress.

6. Have your help and encouragement in overcoming his limitations and improving his abilities so that he can qualify for future increases in pay and responsibilities.

7. Find out how you are doing as a supervisor in terms of availability, understanding, organizing, delegating and the like.

7. Point out the barriers to his doing a good job imposed by your methods of supervision.

The "Fringe" Benefits

Employee benefits have assumed increasing importance in the eyes of employees since the end of World War II. In general, they consist of job rewards over and above pay which are paid for partly or in full by the employer.

Required benefits include social security contributions, workman's compensation and unemployment payments.

Medical and hospitalization insurance is probably the most common benefit provided at the employer's option.

Life insurance plans usually base the amount of their coverage on the employee's salary, one year's earnings being typical. In recent years, instead of the lower cost term insurance, companies have been providing employees with cash value permanent policies which the employee can take over if he leaves the company.

Disability insurance over and above workman's compensation payments—pay continuance coverage—pays covered employees tax-free benefits for illness or injury on or off the job. It can pay for the duration of the disability or for a specified time, depending on the policy. Employers purchasing this type of coverage are spared the agony of deciding how long to keep a disabled employee on salary.

Pensions for employees can be funded as a tax-deductible business expense with Internal Revenue Service approval of the plan. Contributions for each employee must be in ratio to his earnings to qualify. Most pension plans include a death benefit in case the employee dies before retirement and must now provide for vesting—a provision which allows the employee to retain his right to a pension, after he has completed a specified number of years under the plan, even if he leaves the company.

Self-employed retirement plans can also provide employee benefits. A self-employed person—such as the owner-operator of a small motel—is allowed to put 15 percent of his annual income or $7,500 (whichever is less) into a retirement plan for himself and claim a current tax deduction for that amount. Employers taking advantage of this opportunity must also cover all full-time employees during the first three years of employment depending on how the plan is set up.

Profit-sharing plans, as distinguished from annual bonuses, are generally similar to pension plans, except that instead of a fixed annual contribution by the employer the amount paid into the plan is geared to profits for each year.

Deferred compensation is a benefit provided key employees which is a form of retirement plan. Under this arrangement, payment of a portion of the employee's compensation is postponed to a future date (when the employee would probably be in a lower tax bracket). It is conditioned upon the employee continuing to work for the employer for a specified time. The plan does not have to cover all employees—only those selected by the employer—and there is no formula calling for a specific percentage contribution.

Savings plans allow employees to authorize deductions of a limited percentage of their pay for the purchase of savings bonds or company stock with the company matching the deduction in full or in part.

Unfortunately, the cost of employee benefits is much more apparent to the employer than to the employee. An annual review with each employee of his stake in company benefits—which may run from 20 to 30 percent of salary—is good practice, not only to insure appreciation of their value, but also to make certain that they are adequate and being administered efficiently.

Fairness and consistency should be the watchwords in administering the employee relations program. In addition to being good policy, they will help protect management against charges of violating laws prohibiting discrimination against union activities or on the basis of race, color, creed, age, sex or national origin, or violation of a provision of a labor contract if the property deals with a union or unions. Fair and consistent application and interpretation of personnel policies are not only important in respect to handling layoffs, promotions and transfers, but are necessary as well in dealing with discipline and discharge of employees.

Unions Are a "Fact of Life" in Hospitality Business

The lodging industry is, of course, labor intensive. Predictably, it is also substantially unionized, particularly in the larger cities.

Multi-employer bargaining by a committee set up from within the local hotel/motel association is characteristic.

The Hotel & Restaurant Employees and Bartenders International Union (AFL-CIO) claims nearly 500,000 members, a substantial number of whom are drawn from restaurants rather than hotels and motels. It is the only union serving the majority of hotel-motel employees, although the lodging industry also has a limited number of contracts with crafts unions, the Building Service Employees International Union (AFL-CIO) and the International Union of Operating Engineers (AFL-CIO). HRE, claiming exclusive jurisdictional rights to all household and service workers in the hotel industry, is the tenth largest union in the country and the largest service-trades union, according to the Bureau of Labor Statistics. About half its membership is concentrated in the states of New York and California.

While the Bureau of Labor Statistics "estimates that about 50 to 60 percent of the hotel workers are organized," Dr. John Henderson of Michigan State University declares "no one knows the degree of unionization in the lodging industry, neither the unions nor the various hotel and motel associations, nor the BLS, nor the author of this volume."[2]

Keeping a Union at Arm's Length

Although it might seem that an employer offering competitive pay, good benefits and working conditions, as well as enlightened management practices, would be immune to unionization, such is not the case. He also has to conduct effective two-way communication with employees to get credit for the good jobs he provides and to provide an outlet for employees to express their job frustrations and dissatisfactions.

Spelling out and abiding by fair-minded personnel policies can help stave off unionization. At the least, enlightened hotel/motel management should provide these assurances to employees:

1. *Fair treatment.* Every employee shall be treated fairly regardless of race, sex, age, color or creed.
2. *Selection and assignment.* Employees shall be assigned to jobs for which their aptitude and experience best fit them, and to the kind of work which will offer

[2]John P. Henderson, *Labor Market Institutions and Wages in the Lodging Industry* (East Lansing: Michigan State University, 1965), p. 136.

opportunity for maximum growth and advancement. In filling vacancies, the primary aim shall be to select the person best qualified for the job.

3. *Compensation.* Employees shall be compensated equitably for work performed. Appropriate consideration shall be given to general business conditions and pay and benefits for comparable work offered by other companies in the community.

4. *Advancement.* Wherever possible, qualified present employees will be given first consideration for vacancies to which they could be promoted before applicants from outside the organization are considered.

5. *Training.* Every effort will be made to help employees improve their ability to handle their present job and to upgrade their skills for future advancement.

6. *Communication.* Employees shall be fully and promptly informed about policies and plans affecting them and their work. Full opportunity shall be given employees to express themselves on their jobs and relationships within the organization as well as to suggest improvements in work methods and working conditions. Management shall make a continuous effort to learn of and consider employee interests, ideas and attitudes.

7. *Grievances.* Employees shall be given a full and fair hearing on their grievances.

8. *Job security.* Every effort shall be made to provide steady work and continuous employment.

9. *Health and safety.* Management shall insure that work places and working conditions shall be such as to protect employee health and to prevent injury.

10. *Dismissal or lack of advancement.* Every employee shall be told frankly and fully the reasons for his failure to succeed with the organization.

When a Union Organizer Appears

Given the history and present status of the hotel/motel business, chances are that sooner or later a union organizer will be knocking at your door—if he doesn't already have his feet up on your desk! Your most effective strategy to counter a union drive is prompt action . . . based on accurate information and careful planning! By all means seek legal advice from a lawyer knowledgeable in labor matters before you make a move. Labor law is constantly changing and expert guidance is required to avoid the pitfalls you will encounter in dealing with an experienced labor organizer.

Generally, you will receive very little warning that a union is trying to organize your employees. As soon as you suspect that an organization attempt is underway—and after contacting your labor lawyer—check to be sure your personnel policies are being fairly and fully implemented. Be particularly watchful for the following:

- festering employee grievances
- favoritism
- poor morale
- lagging wages and benefits
- deteriorating working conditions
- capricious disciplinary actions
- lack of recognition

Communication Is Crucial

Be prepared to counter in oral and written communications to employees the organizer's main arguments for union membership:

1. Job security.
2. Improved wages and benefits.
3. Representation on grievances.
4. Participation in management.

In waging a campaign against unionization it is particularly important to avoid any statements or actions by management which could be construed either as a threat or a promise. Among the things you may write or say to employees are these:

You may emphasize your belief and your opinion that the people do not need a union; you may talk about the loss of their independence. You may emphasize that an outsider will come between the employee and you. You may state that without a union your door is always open.

You may refer to the cost of union initiation fees, dues and assessments.

You may state your personal opinion concerning the union organizers, providing you do not exceed the legal bounds of libel and slander.

You may express openly the hope that your employees vote against this or any union.

You may remind the employees that they have a right either to join or refrain from joining the union.

You may remind your employees that they do not have to vote for the union because they have signed a membership card.

You may describe the good features of working for you—job opportunities, longevity, job security, steady work.

You may state that the union cannot guarantee additional pay.

You may state that the union cannot guarantee the security and success of the business.

You may discuss the possibility of strikes and serving in picket lines, and you may review the history of the particular union as to such matters.

You may describe the experiences which other employers have had with this or other unions, including those in your own community.

You may urge all employees to vote.

You may call attention to any union falsehoods.

You may explain the meaning of check-off and union shop and the effect they may have on all employees.

Beware These Pitfalls

Unless you want to run afoul of the National Labor Relations Board, be on your guard against these prohibited activities while a union organizing effort is being made.

- offering wage increases or other inducements to employees unless the increases are part of an established pattern.

- threats to fire, suspend or otherwise discriminate against an employee for joining or being in favor of a union.
- discharge of an employee for union activity.
- linking promotions or raises to how an employee votes.
- questioning employees on how they intend to vote on union activities.
- holding a straw vote.
- saying or implying that a union victory would result in a strike.
- other actions which your attorney advises you are illegal.

Negotiating a Contract You Can Live With

If, despite your best efforts, your employees choose to have a union represent them, you may find yourself in the position of having to negotiate a contract either individually or as a member of a multi-employer bargaining team. It is vital at this point to keep in mind that the day to start preparing for negotiations on your *next* contract is the day your *present* contract goes into effect. Everything that happens under your present contract may become a factor in your next negotiation. Prior to beginning negotiations you should, of course, (1) study contracts of other organizations which might have a bearing on yours; (2) review wages, benefits, working conditions and personnel practices; and (3) get recommendations from your supervisors.

Successfully concluding contract negotiations rests on adhering to these sound bargaining principles:

1. *Establish a positive bargaining attitude.* The purpose of bargaining should be to reach *agreement* satisfactory to both sides, one that is both fair and honest.
2. *Recognize the point of view and the sincerity of the union bargaining committee.* In the end, this is the group which must accept the agreement.
3. *Provide the bargaining committee with information to change their views* and to help them sell these new ideas to their members.
4. *Keep in mind that management and union representatives see many things in different perspectives.*
5. *Remember that, in bargaining, you get in return exactly what you give.* Don't try to "put something over" on the union committee, indulge in personalities, shout or "lose your cool."
6. *Keep putting the burden of proof on the union.*
7. *Keep negotiations moving and on target.* Avoid getting hung up on technicalities or discussing unrelated subjects.
8. *Keep employees informed on the progress of negotiations.* Let them know that any gains granted were reached by collective agreement rather than forced from a reluctant management by militant union officials.

What to Do If Your Employees Strike

In the event negotiations collapse, or for any of a number of other reasons, the day may come when you'll have to face up to the possibility of a strike. A strike is a test of economic strength, as well as a clash of wills, between management and the union. Strike threats should not be taken lightly as experience shows that it is relatively easy for union officials to get members to walk out and stay out for a reasonable period of time. As in other matters where a union is concerned, no time should be lost in securing the help of a competent labor lawyer.

If, notwithstanding your best efforts, a strike seems inevitable, consideration needs to be given to the following:

- Informing employees of the circumstances and their rights.
- Arranging to keep in operation—delivery of supplies, obtaining replacement employees, security, maintenance, etc..
- Distribution of back pay to strikers.
- Payment of group insurance premiums.
- Handling of unemployment compensation claims.
- Recording incidents during strike.
- Getting community support and adequate police protection.
- In anticipation of the eventual end of the strike—continued employment of replacements, recall of strikers, effect on employee benefits of strike absence, etc..

3

Helping Hotel
and Motel Employees
to Help You

The difference—as much as 20 percent greater productivity—between the run-of-the mill employee and the superior one is largely a matter of motivation. Just as leading a horse to water does not insure that it will drink, so the most carefully planned and implemented recruiting, selection, orientation and training programs provide no guarantee of other than pedestrian employee performance. To stimulate employees to contribute their full skill, care and effort to the enterprise requires that management be knowledgeable about employee needs and desires and that, without being manipulative, it provides the communication, incentives, recognition and rewards to accomplish this objective.

Employees Do Not See Eye to Eye with Management

What complicates the problem of employee motivation is that management and employees have widely disparate views on what individuals want from their jobs. A study by the U. S. Chamber of Commerce on employee priorities in job satisfaction showed that, while management thought material considerations ranked uppermost in the minds of employees, employees themselves rated the psychological satisfactions more important.

As management saw it, the list of priorities was: (1) good pay; (2) job security; (3) promotion and growth; (4) good working conditions; (5) interesting work; (6) company loyalty; (7) tactful discipline; (8) full appreciation of work performed; (9) sympathetic help with personal problems; (10) feeling "in" on things.

Employees, on the other hand, reported that they ranked the priorities as follows: (1)

full appreciation of work performed; (2) feeling "in" on things; (3) sympathetic help on personal problems; (4) job security; (5) good pay; (6) interesting work; (7) promotion and growth; (8) company loyalty to workers; (9) good working conditions; (10) tactful discipline.

The Hierarchy of Needs

Today's employee is a far cry from predecessor generations in terms of values, life style, needs and motivations. He is better educated, more sophisticated, and more demanding. Yet there needs to be recognition that all humans are motivated by what the eminent psychologist Dr. Abraham Maslow has termed a "hierarchy of needs." In his theory of personality and motivation, Dr. Maslow says that man is motivated to reach a certain goal because he has an internally generated *need* to reach it. Human needs, according to Maslow, can be ranked from the most primitive and urgent (physiological needs) to the need for self-actualization at the top of his scale.

The *physiological* needs include food, shelter, warmth, sleep, water, sex and other physical requirements. *Safety* needs embrace freedom from threat of physical injury as well as emotional security. The need for *belongingness and love* derives from the need for relationships with other people and is a *social* need as distinguished from the first two items in Maslow's list which are personal needs. Near the top of the hierarchy is the need for *esteem*—self-respect and the high regard of others. At the apex is the need for *self-actualization,* making the most of one's abilities and talents.

Central to Maslow's theory is the proposition that, until a given need is satisfied, a person is not motivated by a need higher in the Maslow scale. For example, a really hungry man would care far less for maintaining his self-respect than for satisfying his hunger. At the same time, "a satisfied need is no longer a motivator of behavior." The same hungry man, having his appetite satisfied, ceases, at least for the time being, to be motivated by the need for food.

Theory X vs. Theory Y Management

Other behavioral scientists have developed provocative theories relating to employee motivation. Douglas McGregor is known for his Theory X and Theory Y that deal with two sets of fundamental beliefs managers hold about what people are like and which dictate their management style.

A Theory X manager, McGregor says, believes people dislike work and will avoid it if at all possible, shirk responsibility, are unambitious and excessively security conscious. Therefore such employees respond only to threats of punishment, strict control and demanding supervision.

On the other hand, the Theory Y manager has a more positive attitude toward people. He believes that work is a natural and inherently pleasurable activity, that employees can and will provide their own motivation to achieve organizational objectives, that they seek rather than avoid responsibility, and that they have vast resources of ambition, imagination and creativity which most organizations and managers fail to tap effectively.

McGregor asserts that the Theory Y employee is self-motivated and that his needs can best be met by working toward fulfillment of the organization's goals. Of the two theories and the management strategies evoked by each, McGregor obviously favors Theory Y and the more permissive supervisory style it engenders.

Organization Development Approach

As an outgrowth of the work of Maslow, McGregor, and other behavioral scientists, a new approach, *organization development*, has attracted considerable attention. It is, according to the NTL Institute for Applied Behavioral Science, a way of looking at the whole human side of organizational life. Building on the conviction of many behavioral scientists that our organizations are inefficient in realizing the potential of their human resources, that they function on the basis of incorrect assumptions about the nature of man, and that they tend to limit the growth of the persons who work in them, organization development attempts to integrate individual needs for growth and development with organizational goals and objectives.

Among the behavioral science findings and the theories that support the organizational development—OD—approach are these:

"—Work which is organized to meet people's needs as well as to achieve organizational requirements tends to produce the highest productivity and quality of production.
"—Individuals whose basic needs are taken care of do not seek a soft and secure environment. They are interested in work, challenge, and responsibility. They expect recognition and satisfying interpersonal relationships.
"—People have a drive toward growth and self-realization.
"—Persons in groups which go through a managed process of increasing openness about both positive and negative feelings develop a strong identification with the goals of the group and its other members. The group becomes increasingly capable of dealing constructively with potentially disruptive issues.
"—Personal growth is facilitated by a relationship which is honest, caring, and non-manipulative.
"—Positive change flows naturally from groups which feel a common identification and an ability to influence their environment."

Strategy for Releasing Human Potential

Based on these ideas, OD seeks to identify and overcome the problems that prevent the release of human potential within the organization. An OD project has the following among its objectives:

"1. To create an open, problem-solving climate throughout the organization.

"2. To supplement the authority associated with role or status with the authority of knowledge and competence.

"3. To locate decision-making and problem-solving responsibilities as close to the information sources as possible.

"4. To build trust among individuals and groups throughout the organization.

"5. To make competition more relevant to work goals and to maximize collaborative efforts.

"6. To develop a reward system which recognizes both achievement of the organization's mission (profits or service) and organization development (growth of people).

"7. To increase the sense of 'ownership' of organization objectives throughout the work force.

"8. To help managers to manage according to relevant objectives rather than according to 'past practices' or according to objectives which do not make sense for one's area of responsibility.

"9. To increase self-control and self-direction for people within the organization."

Awareness and Managerial Style

Sensitivity training and the Managerial Grid® are two of the techniques or approaches most frequently used in organizational development programs. Sensitivity training is designed to impart a heightened awareness of the impact of one's behavior on others, as well as increased sensitivity to one's own behavior and the behavior of others. This is usually done through some form of laboratory or group process training. The Managerial Grid® is an outgrowth of sensitivity training which graphically depicts managerial style in respect to relative concern for people and production. Dr. Robert R. Blake, who developed the Grid in conjunction with Dr. Jane S. Mouton, feels that managerial concern for people and concern for production need not be mutually exclusive, but rather are complementary.

The Managerial Grid® enables an individual to evaluate his managerial style on a scale ranging from entirely production oriented to entirely people oriented. Most managers bracket the extremes, but the Grid helps them identify any pronounced deviation either way. The underlying purpose of the Managerial Grid® exercise is to stimulate the manager to consider the implications of his managerial style and to initiate the personal and organizational changes required to improve himself as a manager and to better the climate of the organization.

Significantly, while the Grid provides for extremes of people or production orientation, it also shows up the manager who has little concern for either production or people. The goal of Managerial Grid Training is to produce managers who combine an optimum concern for production with an optimum concern for people since Grid theory views both concerns as interdependent.

The Managerial Grid® has been described as a key for mobilizing human effort and for getting the maximum performance results of which people in industrial life are capable. Through its application, a manager may be able to unleash and utilize creative energy of the kind needed to become and remain competitive in this era of innovation and change.

The Managerial Grid® is not merely a theory or formula. It is a tested system which has been applied in industry and which in each case has contributed significantly to increased profits. One large industrial complex attributed 30 percent of its profit increase directly to the Managerial Grid® and its organization development work.

Sonesta Hotels was one of the first in the lodging industry to expose its top management group to Managerial Grid® training. Since that time there have been other hotel corporations such as Marriott and Howard Johnson's which have applied Grid training to their organizations.

The Managerial Grid®[1]

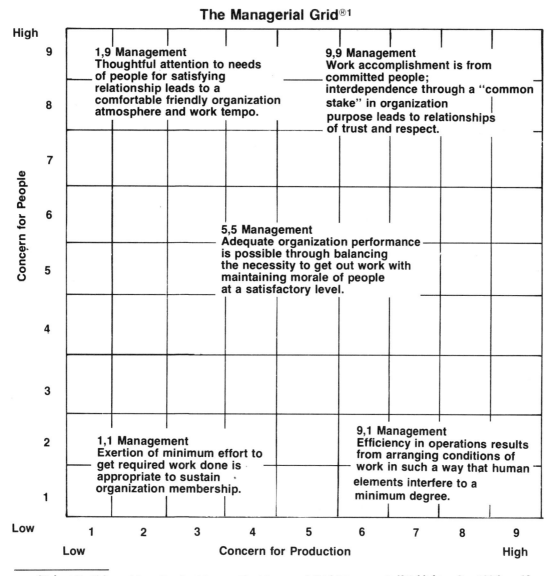

[1]Robert R. Blake and Jane Srygley Mouton, *The Managerial Grid* (Houston: Gulf Publishing Co., 1964), p. 10.

How to Make Employees Team Players

The art of releasing human potential, or helping employees to help you, rests on the foundation of behavioral science. Yet it is not so esoteric an area as to require an in-depth knowledge of psychology and related disciplines in order to achieve worthwhile, sometimes even spectacular, results.

Mel Sandler, head of the hotel department at the University of New Hampshire, asserts that significant gains in employee productivity can be accomplished by making each employee feel he is part of the team. This begins, Sandler says, by achieving an understanding with the employee of what you expect of him and how you will evaluate his performance. Second, he advises, the employee must be shown how his job fits into the "big picture," how his contribution can have an important influence on the success of the whole operation. Finally, Sandler suggests management must supplement effective training programs with coaching, encouragement, challenging and mind-stretching assignments, and constructive discipline when necessary.

Job dissatisfaction, according to Sandler, results when employees are not able to meet the requirements of the job, don't understand its goals, fail to see opportunity for influencing their own progress, and are unable to discuss their discontent with supervisors. The remedy, he says, is discerning and demanding *selection*, sympathetic and comprehensive *orientation* and continuing open two-way *communication*.

Why Employees Quit

Employee turnover—ranging in cost from hundreds to thousands of dollars per employee depending on job level involved—is even more costly than the drain on profits and morale of poorly motivated employees who remain on the payroll. While salaries which are not competitive, or niggardliness in giving raises, sometimes cause valued employees to leave an organization, the reasons far more frequently are non-material.

Lack of recognition, lack of advancement, oversupervision and assignments for which the employee is either over-qualified or underqualified are among the more common reasons why employees quit.

Ingredients of Sound Employee Relations

Sound employee relations are based on a good job environment and effective leadership. The following check list spells out the essential ingredients:

1. A competitive pay structure and benefits package.
2. Safe, comfortable and pleasant working conditions.
3. A communication network which lets employees know what is going on, their part in and benefits from this, what exactly is expected from them, and which provides structured opportunities for upward communication.

4. Particularly in a non-union situation, an opportunity for employees to discuss their problems with levels of supervision higher than their immediate boss.
5. Social and recreational programs to allow employees to associate the organization with pleasure as well as work.
6. Delegation of decision-making authority to the lowest practical level to encourage a sense of participation and involvement among all employees. Authority commensurate with responsibility.
7. Recognition of achievement, at performance appraisal discussions, certainly, but also informally by a pat on the back or a word of commendation for a job well done. Recognition by the peer group is also important, so every opportunity should be taken to let his fellows know of significant accomplishments or milestones in the career of an employee.
8. Training and development opportunities to help employees do their present job better and to prepare them for future growth.

In a nutshell, motivating employees to high performance levels is a function of enlightened company employee relations policies and practices, good supervision, an effective communication system and well planned training programs. The first two of these requirements have already been touched upon.

The Part Communication Plays

Communication involves both structure and process. In a business organization, communication, as defined by the author in an earlier book, is "that interchange of facts, viewpoints and ideas which brings about unity of interest, unity of purpose, and unity of effort in a group of individuals organized to achieve a specific mission. The specific goal of all employee communication efforts is to achieve mutual confidence and understanding between employees and management on all matters of common concern, so that employees will eagerly and enthusiastically support all actions essential to the success of the business.[2]

Since communication is a two-way street, there must be, along with the usual management-to-employee communication channels, opportunities for employees to communicate upward. In addition to providing management with information needed for decision-making, the existence of upward communication channels helps employees relieve the pressures and frustrations of the work situation and enhance their sense of participation in the enterprise. Among the channels and media of upward communication which merit consideration are these: employee attitude surveys, personal contacts by supervisors and managers, informal grievance procedure for non-organized employees, meetings, exit and transfer interviews, performance appraisal discussions, and a question box or "rumor clinic" variant of the suggestion system.

---

[2]Scholz, *op. cit.*, p. 19.

Choosing Appropriate Communication Media

The most important single concept underlying effective communication, be it downward, upward or laterally, is this: *In the final analysis, communication exists only when a person has received what the sender has tried to convey.*

In considering the choice of which among the many available media of downward communication to use in a particular situation or organization, it is worthy of note that people generally remember—

10% of what they *Read*
20% of what they *Hear*
30% of what they *See*
50% of what they *Hear* and *See*
70% of what they *Say*, and
90% of what they *Say* as they *Do* a thing

Following is a sampling of downward communication media appropriate for hotels and motels:

Written
>   Policies, procedures and reports
>   Bulletins
>   Employee publication
>   Letters to employees' homes
>   Literature racks
>   Bulletin Boards
>   Reports to employees

Oral
>   Regular staff and informative meetings
>   Orientation
>   Assignment giving
>   Performance appraisals
>   Counseling
>   Walking the shop and office

How to Give Orders

Inadequate order giving ability on the part of managers and supervisors is a prime source of wasted time and money, as well as a cause of frustration, in most business organizations. Social scientists who have studied the assignment giving procedure of successful leaders offer these suggestions:

1. Make sure the employee is qualified, that the whole task is not beyond his capabilities.
2. Tell the employee the problem to be solved or the objective to be reached.

3. Ask him to suggest the best way of reaching the objective.
4. Make clear when the job must be completed, and why, but ask the employee what problems he may encounter in getting it done on time.
5. Make clear when you want him to check back with you.
6. Specify the limits of his authority.
7. Invite him to come to you if he runs into trouble and needs help.

Suggestion System Stimulates Productivity

Suggestion systems, frequently an important factor in motivating employees to greater involvement and higher productivity, have these characteristics if they are effectively conducted:

1. *They pay off.* Not only in worth-while awards to suggestors, but also in significant dollars-and-cents savings to management as well as improvements in areas such as the quality of the product or service and employee safety.
2. *They encourage participation.* Obviously the more suggestions, the greater the likelihood of getting a real "winner."
3. *They are purposive.* They are oriented toward helping management achieve its goals and objectives.
4. *They are efficient.* Every suggestion submitted is given prompt, fair evaluation.

Planning a Training Program

Employee training and its kissin' cousin, management development, are key elements in creating and maintaining an effective work force. They are no panaceas, however, since high morale and strong motivation derive from a broad spectrum of organizational policies and practices. As a matter of fact, as Washington columnist William Raspberry puts it, "education is the solution only to the degree that ignorance is the problem."

In planning a training program a number of questions need to be answered such as—

What should be taught?
When should training take place?
Where should training be done?
How should it be done?
Who should be the trainer?
How much training should there be?
How will the training be measured?

In planning and administering a training program it is essential to keep in mind the six *basic principles of learning.*

1. *Motivation*—preliminary to any training situation is the necessity to create a

desire to learn on the part of the employee. Motivation, as has been emphasized earlier, is not necessarily primarily material.

2. *Objective*—learning is more rapid and complete when one knows exactly what he is expected to learn as well as the purpose of the exercise.
3. *Doing*—the best learning occurs when the student actually performs the operation.
4. *Realism*—the more realistic the situation, the more efficient the learning process.
5. *Background*—new learning is best based on past knowledge or experience.
6. *Appreciation*—learning is facilitated by showing the student how what he is being taught has practical application in his daily life and on the job, as well as by pointing out the direct benefits he may enjoy as a result of his newly acquired knowledge or skill.

Orientation Is the First Step

Employee training begins with the *orientation* of new hires. Included in this phase of the training program should be:

A. Brief history of the organization.
B. Philosophy of operation and broad policies which govern practices.
C. General outline of the job, working relationships and the name of employee's supervisor if the supervisor has not already met him in the selection process.
D. Information on pay and payday, hours, holidays, benefit programs, etc.
E. A description of the organization and communication network—chain of command.
F. A tour of the operation, including introduction to fellow employees.

The Mechanics of a Training Program

On-the-job training follows the basic steps of Motivation, Explanation, Demonstration, Application, Examination and Follow-up Supervision. An excellent source of detailed information on the conduct of on-the-job training is the American Management Association reprint, "On-the-Job Training: Making the Most of Manpower."*

In general, training programs should include:

A. The objective of the training, what will be expected of the students and procedures to be followed.
B. Presentation of instruction by lecture and demonstration or other training techniques with emphasis on the "why" as well as the "how."
C. Application of the new information or skill by the student through one or several of the following techniques:
    1. Group performance or controlled practice.
    2. Independent practice allowing each student to proceed at his own pace.
    3. Coach-and-pupil method in which paired students alternate roles.

*American Management Association Reprint Service, 135 West 50th Street, New York, N. Y. 10020.

    4. In supervisory and management training, the use of role playing, "in-basket"* and similar exercises.
  D. Examination (often the application phase suffices).
  E. Review and follow-up.

During World War II the Training Within Industry programs developed a four-step job instruction method which is as valid today as it was then.

HOW TO INSTRUCT

Step One—*Explanation*
    Put trainee at ease
    Describe job, its purpose and importance

Step Two—*Demonstration*
    Show how to do job, step-by-step
    Stress key points

Step Three—*Application*
    Let trainee do job, explaining steps and key points.
    Correct errors, compliment and encourage.

Step Four—*Follow-Up*
    Supervise employee, checking use of new skills from time to time, giving encouragement and inviting questions.

If the student hasn't learned, the teacher hasn't taught.

Numerous aids can be used to dramatize and/or facilitate training. Among them are these:

  Charts and blackboard
  Film strips or slides
  Motion pictures
  Mock-ups or models
  Programmed learning utilizing special textbooks
    or teaching machines
  Closed circuit TV

Audio-visual aids in common use range in complexity and cost but not necessarily in effectiveness from basic slides and artwork at the bottom of the scale to full color videotape at the top. In between, at ascending levels of cost, are the following:

  Film strip (no sound)
  Film strip and record (or audio cassette)
  Cartridge film strip and audio-tape
  8mm. film, in reel or cartridge
  16mm. film (reel)

---

*In-basket is a variation of the traditional case study method utilizing intensive analysis of simulated management problems.

Newer Training Aids Speed Learning

Most innkeepers are familiar with all of the foregoing except, perhaps, videotape and the recently developed Electronic Video Recording. EVR permits the use of one or many standard television sets to display training films any time the viewer wants to see them. With this equipment there's no need to darken the room and no projector noise. Further, the action can be stopped at any time for single-frame viewing. While the current cost of EVR players is relatively high, prices may be expected to come down with volume production. EVR cartridges are already competitive in price.

Programmed learning is a technique of self-instruction which has been widely adopted by many organizations. The underlying theory of this technique is that people learn best when they are called upon for an active response to each new item of information. Argyle Publishing Corp., a leading producer of programmed instruction materials, lists these features of programmed instruction:

"1. Material is broken down into short units called frames.
"2. Each frame requires active responses.
"3. The learner gets immediate feedback on whether he's correct.
"4. Programmed instruction is individualized and self-paced.
"5. Classrooms and scheduled classes are not necessary since programmed instruction is self-instructional.
"6. Programs are pretested and revised to insure that they attain the desired training objectives.
"7. Programmed instruction is often more effective and efficient than traditional forms of instruction."

Audio cassettes are finding more and more acceptance as a training aid by business, especially for management development. Cassettes are produced by banks offering analyses of economic conditions, by trade associations, by management training groups and by organizations wishing to give greater currency to convention presentations or inspirational talks by company executives.

The Fairmont Hotel in Dallas, for example, provides key management people with cassette tape recorders so they can listen to management instructional material while traveling to and from work in their automobiles.

Combine Heart and Head for Improved Productivity

Noted psychologist William James observed some time ago: "The deepest need in human nature is the craving to be appreciated."

Recognition of this need is at the bottom of virtually all successful productivity improvement programs. As the classic Hawthorne studies at a Western Electric plant proved many years ago, simply paying attention to employees can result in surprising incremental improvements in performance.

Little things like providing attractive uniforms, extra amenities and important-sounding titles can improve morale and help raise productivity. Example: the designations "bellhop" or "bellboy" were considered demeaning by most of those occupying the position which has since generally been re-titled "bellman."

A number of hotels and chain operations go out of their way to give recognition to outstanding employees. Marriott, for one, goes to great lengths to make each employee feel that he is important and a valued member of the team. There is some significance to the fact that more winners and top contenders for the AH & MA "Bellman of the Year" contest have come from Marriott properties than any other chain.

Not the least rewarding of Marriott's methods for improving employee productivity is the company's generous profit sharing plan. When a kitchen helper under the plan can look forward to a payoff of more than $100,000 at retirement—and managers can become millionaires—the incentive for outstanding performance has got to be very potent.

In general, however, improved employee productivity hinges on more effective use of the well-known management techniques of Planning, Organizing, Integrating and Measuring.

There is probably not a lodging operation in the country which could not realize at least a 10 percent immediate gain in productivity on many jobs simply by applying the classic *Work Simplification Formula*:

1. Select a job to improve
2. Get the facts—make a process chart
3. Challenge every detail—list the possibilities
4. Develop the preferred method
5. Install the improvements; check results.

4

The Business of People Pleasing: Practical Ways to Accommodate Hotel and Motel Guests

"Let's be sure that everyone enjoys the same personal warmth he would expect as a guest in our own home." That is the guiding philosophy of the Dunfey Family Hotels, New England's largest innkeeper.

As enunciated by Mrs. Catherine A. Dunfey, Chairman of the Board, it explains how five of her eight sons progressed in a time span of less than 15 years from a rented food concession at Hampton Beach, New Hampshire, to operators of a chain of hotels and motels stretching from Portland, Maine, to San Francisco, California.

In the final analysis, innkeeping is the art of pleasing people. It involves, of course, providing clean, comfortable accommodations and appetizing food and drink. But more than that, it requires a certain graciousness in service, an attention to details and a dedicated effort to minimize annoyances to guests. (See Figure 4-1, page 62, for example.)

What Guests Want

A survey of guests patronizing the nation's best known chain hotels and motels disclosed that "overall cleanliness, reasonable prices and comfort," as one might expect, outranked all other considerations in determining choice of accommodations. But next in importance was "courtesy of staff." And high on the list were "people pleasing" items such as "ease of getting reservations," "ease of checking in and checking out" and "atmosphere."

AT THE CHASE-PARK PLAZA WE DON'T REST ON OUR LAURELS. WE'RE CONTINUALLY TRYING TO LIVE UP TO OUR REPUTATION AS "AMERICA'S FINEST HOTEL". IF WE FAIL IN ANY OF THE FOLLOWING AREAS, WE INVITE YOU TO BE OUR GUEST FOR THE DRINK OF YOUR CHOICE.

1 If the doorman fails to provide the attention and courtesy you deserve.

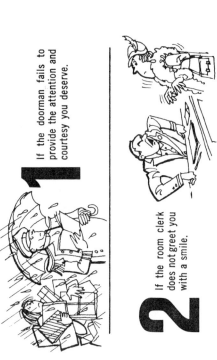

2 If the room clerk does not greet you with a smile.

3 If the bellman fails to courteously deliver your baggage to your accommodations within 10 minutes after you are assigned to your room, and neglects to courteously show you our various services and their operation.

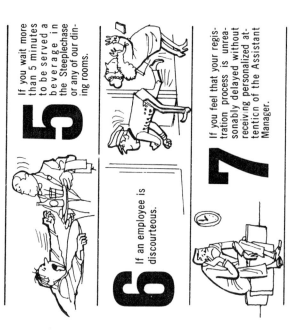

4 If your Continental Breakfast is not delivered within 20 minutes after placing your order.

5 If you wait more than 5 minutes to be served a beverage in the Steeplechase or any of our dining rooms.

6 If an employee is discourteous.

7 If you feel that your registration process is unreasonably delayed without receiving personalized attention of the Assistant Manager.

So, if any employee "wears his laurel crown lightly" just ask him for a "chit" that would be good for one drink in any Chase-Park Plaza bar or restaurant. On the other hand, you may wish to save the "chit". We think that they're going to be very, very scarce.

Figure 4-1

Front Office Sets the Tone

The business of people pleasing in a hotel or motel gravitates around the "front office." It is here that guests first form a substantial evaluation of the property and it is also here that they come with their problems or complaints.

Basically, the front office (1) processes reservations and handles communications with prospective guests, (2) registers guests and assigns rooms, (3) handles mail and messages for guests, (4) makes credit arrangements, (5) gives information about shopping, local attractions, etc. to guests, and (6) arranges miscellaneous guest services.

In large properties, the cashiers may report to the controller, but in small hotels and motels receiving guest payments is a front office function.

Processing Reservations

Reservations may come from many sources—by telephone, mail, telegram or in person, from travel agencies, hotel representatives, airlines, referrals from other hotels or motels, and from a reservation system of which the property is a member. Whatever the source, the following steps are required for each reservation:

1. It must be accepted or refused by an authorized person.
2. A confirmation or refusal should be sent to the prospective guest as soon as possible.
3. Involved functions should be notified.
4. Systematic records must be maintained.

Solutions to Reservation Problems

The "Operation Breakthrough" study of the American Hotel & Motel Association stated, "Present reservation procedures in the lodging industry are very time consuming and inconvenient for the customers." Not only, it pointed out, do travelers frequently have to contact a number of hotels or motels in a given city to find available space, but manual reservation systems tend to be error prone.

One approach to solution of the problem which has been suggested is to create area hotel clearing houses as has been done in Jamaica and Bermuda. By gathering and consolidating space availability data for a city or area, prospective guests could be provided with acceptable alternative accommodations if their first choice was sold out.

An electronic system is available in major cities that can immediately indicate vacancies in all member hotels. In the lobby of each participating hotel there is a display board listing all member properties having vacancies. When a prospective guest calls a hotel for a room, and that hotel is full, the clerk simply has to check the display board in order to refer that caller to a hotel or motel having rooms available.

Another development is the automated reservation system. Those operated by a chain for its own properties of course limit the customer's choice to the properties comprising the chain. Even independent reservation service organizations offer limited customer service since they have data on and can make reservations only in subscribing member properties.

Ideally, the total travel package should be available through an integrated reservation system that would enable the traveler to make reservations with one telephone call or at one place for hotel/motel accommodations, airline tickets, car rental, attractions, and other travel services. Progress is being made toward this end.

Reservation systems have both internal and external aspects. The internal function has to do with recordkeeping within the property to maintain room inventories and other guest information. The external reservation system concerns itself with procedures for helping guests make reservations quickly and efficiently.

Cornell Internal Reservation System Concepts

The Cornell University School of Hotel and Restaurant Administration has done considerable developmental work on internal reservation systems. Among the concepts embodied in the Cornell approach are these:

- Reservations are entered, as received, in the hotel's magnetic reservation file.
- As reservations are entered into the hotel's computerized reservation system, the computer prepares form letters of acceptance or rejection containing all pertinent information which are sent to customers for verification.
- Direct communication by remote reservation offices and special travel agents with the hotel's internal reservation system provides for direct processing by the computer system of reservation requests and confirmations with provision for automatic handling of close-out periods, travel agents' commissions, etc.

Computerized Reservation Systems Provide Many Benefits

Among the advantages of a computerized internal reservation system such as Cornell's, can be included:

1. Improved accuracy of reservation information and processing.
2. Rapid information retrieval by desired classification such as "volume of business generated by an agent," "number of cancellations," "percentage of no-shows," etc..
3. Easy detection of duplicate reservations.
4. Fast retrieval of individual reservations.
5. Ability to provide status reports on number of vacant rooms, expected check-outs, number of reservations to be picked up, etc..
6. Minimizing problem of lost reservations.
7. Elimination of multiple handling of individual reservation paperwork.

Considerations in Choosing a Reservation System

Nearly 85 percent of guests in a recent survey stated that it was "important" to have an advance reservation. A slightly higher percentage of those questioned actually had made an advance reservation. The telephone was used by 45 percent of the respondents in making reservations.

Only about 18 percent of reservations are made by guests personally. Secretaries make 25 percent of all reservations and travel agencies, airlines, corporate travel departments, other hotels, etc., account for 57 percent.

There are undeniable advantages to making use of some type of reservation service. Competing services claim to excel on some or all counts. In evaluating what a particular reservation service can do for your property, consideration should be given to factors such as these:

Capacity of system to store hotel/motel availability data.

Exposure and availability of system to users—number of reservation centers and terminals on line.

Performance—quality of service, accuracy of billing, user satisfaction, value of service to the hotel or motel.

Once a decision has been reached on *which* service—or services—to affiliate with, the next question is whether or not to obtain a terminal. The answer depends on the number of reservations the hotel/motel might reasonably expect the reservation service to generate. If a property expects less than 50 reservations a month from this source, it would be well advised to seek maximum exposure at minimum cost by using more than one reservation service and postponing installation of a terminal. As a rule of thumb, if 100 or more reservations a month can be expected from a reservation service, serious consideration should be given to acquiring its terminal.

Coping with Check-in and Check-out Problems

A major source of irritation for hotel/motel users, and of frustration for innkeepers, is the queuing up often encountered during check-in and check-out, particularly at those properties catering to conventions and large business meetings.

Barron Hilton, President of Hilton Hotels Corporation, has characterized check-in and check-out procedures of most hotels as "the Achilles heel of the hotel industry." Registration problems and delays can result from:

- inadequate or inaccurate room availability data
- misplaced or lost reservations
- time consumed in filling out forms by both the guest and the front desk clerk.

Similarly in the check-out process, inadequate, inaccurate or delayed data on guest charges result in sometimes unconscionable delays.

Automated procedures such as those in the Cornell Integrated Hotel Management

System should go a long way toward eliminating registration and check-out problems by reducing clerical effort and improving both the timeliness and accuracy of information.

Under the Cornell System, the same guest data put into the computer when a reservation is made is retrieved for use in registering the guest when he checks in. At this time an on-line computer guest ledger record is set up which can instantaneously record room, food and beverage, laundry, valet and even telephone charges. When the guest checks out, a complete and up-to-the-minute statement is immediately retrievable from the computer.

It has been estimated that the Cornell System—which embraces payroll, accounts payable, accounts receivable, purchasing, inventory control, guest history, internal reservations, food control and guest billing—can reduce labor and equipment costs by $5 a month per room.

Proposed Solutions

Among the solutions for registration and check-out problems which have been proposed, and some of which are provided in the Cornell System, are the following:

1. Integration of registration with the reservation system.
2. Automatic accumulation and verification of all guest charges as incurred.
3. Establishment of segregated check-in points by type of guest—confirmed reservations, walk-in, conventions, etc..
4. Use of a roving expediter in registration area to prevent or overcome bottlenecks.
5. Increase in number of registration and check-out stations, particularly during periods of peak activity, with billing data available at *all* check-out stations rather than having stations service only certain floors.
6. Provision for separating the handling of guests and their luggage, possibly by making self-service luggage carts available or by arranging for direct delivery of luggage from airport to hotel room.
7. Use of a uniform, machine readable guest identification card for reservations and registration.
8. Pre-registration of guests arriving in groups or holding confirmed guaranteed reservations.

An approach to speeding check-outs which is used by several major chains, particularly with convention groups, consists simply of providing guests with a "VIP Check-out" form which they fill in with billing information and leave, along with their room key, when they end their stay.

What Price Overbooking?

Related to the reservation problem is an even larger one—that of "overbooking." At certain times and certain places it has caused considerable inconvenience and often extra expense to holders of confirmed reservations. It has also resulted in litigation and some stiff judgments against offending hotels.

Despite the common use by other industries of mathematical forecasting techniques for planning purposes, it has been pointed out that the lodging industry still adheres largely to a "seat of the pants" approach in deciding how many reservations to accept for future occupancy. Guided by the philosophy that "There is no commodity more perishable than a hotel room. If it is not sold tonight, it can never be sold," innkeepers play daily Russian Roulette with their advance bookings in an effort to insure close to 100 percent occupancy in the face of actual nationwide average occupancy in the neighborhood of 70 percent.

Since it can be expected, based on past experience, that about five percent of those making reservations will be "no-shows" and about 10 percent will cancel, the usual practice is to overbook by around 10 percent. This figure takes into consideration the five percent of guests who remain beyond their originally planned departure date. Postponement of athletic events such as an outdoor fight or World Series game, or an unexpected snow storm can play havoc with the percentages as can variations from the average number of cancellations and "no shows."

When an overbooking situation develops, it is important not only to treat the traveler with the utmost courtesy and consideration, but also to help him obtain alternate accommodations until a room is available in the property of his first choice.

Western International was the first hotel chain to offer certified reservations. Under this plan, if a room is not available for a guest who has made a reservation, a room in another hotel is found and the Western International hotel pays for the room and round trip cab fare as well.

Electronics to the Rescue

The magic of electronics can be of considerable help in overcoming reservations problems. Systems are available which are designed to avoid overbooking, underselling and incorrect rates through electronic room inventory control and reservation processing. Among the advantages of such systems are accurate and uniform inventory information, elimination of errors and confusion and instant automatic updating every time a reservation is processed.

Likewise, electronic management control systems can tell the front desk and housekeeper instantly without verbal communication, which rooms are vacant, occupied or being cleaned. By use of a console of lights and switches, they also enable the front desk to instruct housekeeping to clean a particular room and allow the housekeeper to know where her maids are working, as well as room status.

Credit Cards—Sooner or Later

The continuing trend toward a "cashless" economy in the U. S. puts a premium on a progressive approach to credit card acceptance by innkeepers. Subject to the usual caveats concerning identification and verification, a liberal policy on credit cards can make a significant contribution to hotel/motel profits. It can also go a long way toward improving guest relations and speeding registration and check out.

To be balanced against the cost of honoring credit cards are considerations such as these:

> A number of travelers are uneasy about carrying large sums of cash or even travelers checks. They seek out accommodations which will accept their credit card.
>
> Many businessmen insist on using credit cards because they can use the monthly statement for tax or expense account purposes rather than accumulating a drawer full of receipted bills.
>
> People using credit cards are ipso facto believers in the "consume now-pay later" philosophy. They are therefore less likely to be inhibited in their spending.
>
> Credit card users are a group which ranks high in education and affluence. They are generally in the age bracket which travels and spends more than either the young or the elderly.

Some properties, while recognizing credit cards, suggest that they be used for identification only and that the guest allow the hotel or motel to bill them directly at home. In this way, the property has a means of establishing the credit rating of the guest before extending credit yet is able to save the credit charge. Of course, bad debts and the cost of billing direct may outweigh any potential saving on credit card charges.

If Telephone Problems "Bug" You . . .

A frequent cause of guest complaints is poor telephone service in the hotel or motel.

The story, probably apocryphal, is told of a guest at a particular property who, on checking out, gave the cashier a $20 bill and instructed her to buy some flowers for the telephone switchboard operator.

"Why, that's very thoughtful of you, sir," the cashier said. "I'm sure she'll be glad to know you appreciated her effort to serve you efficiently." "Service, hell," the guest exploded. "I thought she was dead!"

To test the telephone efficiency of your property, pick a peak traffic time and call the switchboard from outside. If any of the following occurs, you've got trouble.

1. Continual "busy" signals
2. Slow response
3. Long delays in completing calls
4. Poor telephone manners

Among the remedies for these problems are:

1. Addition of one or more trunk lines or rearranging trunks to be more in line with

incoming-outgoing call requirements. Your telephone company will review your needs.

2. Take advantage of free telephone company operator training instruction and printed materials covering switchboard procedure and telephone manners.
3. Utilize time-saving switchboard equipment such as automatic continuous ringing.
4. Make it easy for operators to get room information, either by locating records near the switchboard or by an arrangement which assures quick access to needed data.

5

Money-Saving Ideas
on Hotel and Motel
Maintenance and Housekeeping

Together, the engineering/maintenance department and the housekeeping department are responsible for cleaning, upkeep, repair, replacement, installation and maintenance of the property and its furnishings, machinery and equipment.

Under maintenance/engineering fall these types of work:

A. General maintenance and repair, including structural maintenance, grounds and swimming pool care and such tasks as heavy cleaning, carpet servicing, furniture moving, trash removal, minor repairs, maintenance of cleaning and other tools and equipment used by the department. It might also include painting, upholstering and cabinet making.
B. Maintenance of heating, ventilating, refrigerating and air conditioning systems.
C. Maintenance of electrical, radio and television and communication systems.
D. Maintenance of motors and electrical appliances.
E. Maintenance of water supply, plumbing fixtures and the sewage system.
F. Fire protection and prevention, including maintenance of fire equipment and establishment of fire protection procedures.

R & M Costs Are Substantial

Repair and maintenance costs can be a sizeable item for a hotel or motel. According to a study made by Harris, Kerr, Forster, they run well over $400 per available room. It needs to be remembered, however, that this figure, conforming to the Uniform System of Accounts for Hotels, includes not only repair and maintenance expenditures for guest rooms but also for public rooms, dining rooms, kitchen, mechanical and climate control equipment and the structure itself. It also includes wages and salaries of maintenance personnel. And this is an important factor, for there has been a constant rise in the costs of labor and materials going into maintenance and repair work. As might be expected, larger hotels generally have higher repair and maintenance costs per available room due to higher rates charged, more services offered and greater proportion of public space.

The greater proportion of maintenance money, at least so far as motels are concerned, goes for equipment (2.2%). In relation to sales, this is how maintenance money is spent, according to a study of motels with restaurants by Laventhol, Krekstein, Horwath and Horwath:

> Equipment 2.2%
> Furnishings .9%
> Building .8%
> Painting and Decorating .7%
> Grounds .5%
> Miscellaneous .3%
> Swimming pool .1%
> Total repairs and maintenance 5.5% of sales.

The key, of course, to keeping the property up and repair and maintenance costs down is a systematic approach involving preventive maintenance and periodic routine inspection and repair. An excellent guide is Thomas Sack's *Complete Guide to Building and Plant Maintenance, Second Ed.*, published by Prentice-Hall, Inc.

How Sheraton Corporation Handles Maintenance

Sheraton Corporation has developed a unique Maintenance Request System which is claimed to eliminate most causes of guest complaints before the problem comes up and to insure prompt response to guest complaints due to maintenance problems. Before the system was installed by Sheraton it was evaluated by chief engineers representing more than 60 hotels ranging in size from 100 to 1,500 rooms.

Among the advantages claimed for this system are that it:

- provides a complete record of each problem from report to solution
- reduces oral requests and assignments
- is easily understood
- permits screening of requests
- eliminates duplication of effort and records
- reveals staffing problems
- ties inspection in with repair call

Specially designed three-page maintenance request forms show:

1. date of request for work

2. person or department requesting
3. description of problem
4. to whom assigned
5. when completed
6. time spent on work
7. remarks by person doing the work

The back of the third form contains a check list of things to be inspected while on the primary service call.

Maintenance Request Procedure

1. The originator of a maintenance request fills out the three-page form, keeps the top page (white) and sends the other two to the engineering/maintenance department.

2. Head of department assigns the job and places both copies of the form on the "assignment" hook under the repairman's name.

3. Repairman puts one copy of form (blue) on the "In Process" hook and takes the third copy (on heavier buff stock and with check list on back) along with him to place where repair is to be made. After completing the repair he inspects the area for other maintenance deficiencies as noted in the check list and remedies them, if possible.

4. On returning to the assignment board, employee removes the blue form from the "In Process" hook and staples it to the buff form which he has filled out.

   a. If assigned work has been completed, both tickets are placed on "Complete" hook.
   b. If work couldn't be finished, the reason why is noted and the tickets are put on the "Not Complete" hook.
   c. If a maintenance deficiency was noted, but not corrected, the tickets are placed on the "Complete-Inspection Deficiency" hook.

5. When forms are removed from "Report" section of board, disposition is as follows:

   a. If job is completed, blue copy is sent back to originator of maintenance request.
   b. If problem was not solved, needed materials are secured and the Maintenance Request form is reissued.
   c. If an inspection deficiency was noted and not corrected, a new form is written up and the job assigned to someone with the skills and equipment to do the job.

The "Backlog" section of the assignment board makes it easy to spot when work builds up for a particular trade such as painters or electricians indicating the possible need for additional help or contracting out work of that type.

How to Cut Water Waste

Water will not only erode stone, but *wastage* of water will show up—and much more rapidly—in erosion of hotel/motel profits. Stephen S. J. Hall, a former hotelman now an administrator at Harvard University, suggests the 18 ways which follow to cut water consumption:

1. Make sure the hotel system has cross connections between high and low level services, allowing water from the high level to flow into low level service, and back into the city system.

2. If your establishment has two or more meters connected to the city supply, there should be no cross connections. If pressures in the services differ, even slightly, this could allow water from a higher pressure line to flow back into a lower pressure line and then back into the city supply after being metered. Wherever possible, use one city service, even if a new impeller or a larger pump is necessary to supply house tanks.

3. If tanks are located on the roof, make sure, when an increase in pressure is necessary, that this does not cause the house tank to fill and overflow.

4. If faucets are frequently left open in service and kitchen areas, install pressure-operating faucets.

5. Consider reducing the size of supply lines or installing orifice plates in lines to reduce flow.

6. Explore ways to recapture clean waste water for possible use in the laundry or elsewhere where health department requirements will not be breached.

7. Check all plumbing fixtures frequently for leaks and repair immediately.

8. Where city water is used for condensing of air conditioning and refrigerating compressors, investigate use of cooling tower water for both summer and winter operation. This can save ½ - 2 gallons per operating minute per ton of refrigeration. If it is economically impractical to connect the condensing unit to cooling tower water, regulating valves should be installed and kept accurately adjusted. The water coming from the condenser should approach 95 degrees. Any cooler water indicates waste.

9. Investigate leaks in the laundry and the possibility of using control valves on washers. If control valves have been installed, make sure they are operating properly and are not leaking.

10. When making periodic inspection for leaks in toilet bowls, also be sure that: toilet flushometers are adjusted to allow flushing time of seven seconds. Urinal flushometers should be set to provide a flushing time of 4-5 seconds. Flush tanks should be regulated for 4 gallons per flushing.

11. Make sure that the blow-downs on boilers are not leaking. All possible steam condensate should be returned to boilers. If blow-down valves are leaking or steam condensate is wasted, this means additional make-up water will be needed.

12. Check water softeners to see if use of high capacity resin would produce a savings by reducing the frequency of regenerations.

13. Inspect cooling tower during operation to determine whether the loss of water due to windage is above normal. If tower has exceptionally bad cross draft, it might be desirable to install a wind screen.

14. Packing glands on pumps should be checked frequently for excessive leakage.
15. Make sure that potato peelers are equipped with a solenoid valve to shut the water off when not in use. Garbage disposal units can also be fitted with a solenoid with a time delay to shut the water off a minute or so after the unit is turned off.
16. Check efficiency of hot water circulating systems by noting the time it takes to get hot water from opened tap. If system is faulty or undersized, an excessive amount of water will be run before guests receive hot water.
17. Check make-up tanks to see that they are of proper size. If they are overflowing, either larger or additional ones should be installed.
18. Be aware of your water problems. Log your meters hourly during periods of high and low occupancy and over weekends. What are your periods of peak load? Where is the water going? Attempt to isolate portions of your load. Get the facts.

A test installation of shower flow control valves in 100 guest rooms at the Motor House in Williamsburg, Va. cost about $4 for material and $1 for labor per room. Annual savings per room by reducing shower flow from six gallons a minute to less than half that figure amounted to $7.93 for water and $4.14 for fuel.

Reducing Heating Costs

While he was AH&MA's Engineering Cost Control Consultant, Mr. Hall suggested the following checklist to help reduce heating costs:

1. Take stack measurement of boilers' CO_2 level often; keep record of adjustments required. If you do not have an analyzer, ask your fuel supplier to make the test for you. (If you heat with oil, the boilers' CO_2 level should approach 13 percent. If you heat with gas, the boilers' CO_2 level should be between 10-11 percent.)
2. Check needless loss of condensate; recover it all if you can. Frequently the expense of a condensate storage tank plus piping is less than the cost of fuel saved in heating cold make-up water.
3. Check return water for blowing traps.
4. Use low pressure steam where possible to reduce losses because high pressure systems tend to leak more easily.
5. Insulate all pipes and boilers.
6. Remove unused piping which would otherwise be wasting heat.
7. Consider zoning heating system so that entire building is not heated to satisfy demand in one room or area.
8. Consider separating function room and dining room heating from the guest room heating system.
9. Steam traps should be inspected at least once a year and rebuilt if required.
10. Replace steam pumps with electric.
11. Consider these additional ways to reduce heat loss.

- Keep temperature in unoccupied function and guest rooms at 50-60°F or turn heat off.
- In occupied rooms, keep temperature not more than 72°F.
- Use 100% return air when heating function rooms before use. Shut off outside air intakes used for ventilating when heating unoccupied areas. Fresh air is required only when heating *occupied* space.
- Install vestibules and revolving doors.
- Tighten loose windows and check weather-stripping.
- Stop use of unessential exhaust fans and fresh air fans.

12. Reclaim as much heat as possible from laundry waste water by installing a heat exchanger. The hot waste water will then pre-heat the make-up water for the hot water generator. In hotels which purchase steam, the condensate and/or its heat can often be utilized.

Cutting Fuel Costs

Incomplete combustion in fuel oil fired heating systems can increase fuel bills by as much as 15 percent. The chart below graphically illustrates the cost of incomplete combustion.

SAVINGS FOR EVERY $100 FUEL COSTS BY INCREASE OF COMBUSTION EFFICIENCY

Assuming Constant Radiation and Other Unaccounted for Losses

From an Original Efficiency of:	To an Increased Combustion Efficiency of:								
	55%	60%	65%	70%	75%	80%	85%	90%	95%
50%	$9.10	$16.70	$23.10	$28.60	$33.30	$37.50	$41.20	$44.40	$47.40
55%	—	8.30	15.40	21.50	26.70	31.20	35.30	38.90	42.10
60%	—	—	7.70	14.30	20.00	25.00	29.40	33.30	37.80
65%	—	—	—	7.10	13.30	18.80	23.50	27.80	31.60
70%	—	—	—	—	6.70	12.50	17.60	22.20	26.30
75%	—	—	—	—	—	6.30	11.80	16.70	21.10
80%	—	—	—	—	—	—	5.90	11.10	15.80
85%	—	—	—	—	—	—	—	5.60	10.50
90%	—	—	—	—	—	—	—	—	5.30

Source: American Hotel & Motel Association

On top of higher fuel costs, due to oil not being fully burned, incomplete combustion resulting in an accumulation of soot in the boiler reduces the heating efficiency of the system. The following chart shows how boiler soot can raise fuel bills by nearly 10 percent more.

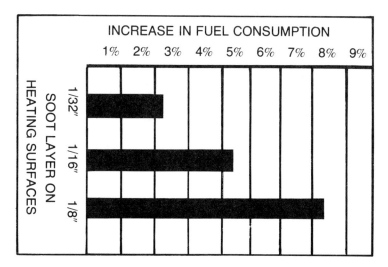

Source: American Hotel & Motel Association.

Combustion engineers suggest the following three simple steps to prevent your heating dollars from going up in smoke.

1. Observe the fuel-air ratio recommended by the burner manufacturer.
2. Keep fuel oil temperature at burner tip at suggested level.
3. Be sure burners are properly adjusted and nozzles clean.

Solving Common Plumbing Problems

Probably the most frequent and frustrating maintenance problems of a hotel/motel have to do with the plumbing system. Here are some suggestions for solving the most common of them.

Ways to Assure Proper Hot Water Temperature

Optimum efficiency from hot water heating equipment can be obtained if it is set to produce water at 135°. Producing water at a higher temperature accelerates problems with valves and washers, to say nothing of being both annoying and potentially dangerous for guests.

Installing a circulating pump on the hot water return line has the effect of making all of the hot water piping in the system a reservoir and improves the availability of hot water for guest use, eliminating the water wasted for the flow of hot water. If the circulating pump still does not help in making the required amount of hot water available, the tubes may need cleaning for increased heat transfer. The only other solution is to get a larger water heater.

Proper Faucet Pressure Cuts Maintenance Costs

Excess pressure at faucets is hard on washers and the rush of water which results when a faucet is turned on can also cause water hammer and sediment filled water. It may be that showers will need slightly higher pressure than sink faucets to operate properly, but experts advise that no more pressure should be provided for shower heads than is actually needed for proper operation.

Following are recommended flow pressures:

Flow Pressure Pounds Per Square Inch

Gauge (absolute pressure)		Flow: Gallons Per Minute
Basin Faucet	8	3.0
Bathtub Faucet	5	6.0
Shower Faucet	12	5.0
Sink Faucet	10	4.5

Minimizing Pipe Corrosion

Regardless of size or age, every hotel or motel has a water pipe corrosion problem, either actual or incipient. Some have had to replace water tubing in as little as five years time due to corrosion. Others have had to install numerous clamps on pipes to stop leaks causing thousands of dollars worth of damage. If your property is located in an area known to have corrosive water, a thorough investigation should immediately be made of the water supply system to determine the rate of corrosion taking place. Motels with pipes embedded in the walls or concrete floors need to be especially alert to the problem of corrosion because the expense of replacing such tubing generally involves major structural and redecorating charges in addition to the expense of the new piping.

Check hot water tubing first because hot water is far more corrosive than cold water. Contrary to general opinion, soft waters are usually more acid and generally have a more corrosive action on the pipes than most hard waters. When repairs or partial replacements are made in plumbing systems, pipes and fittings of the same materials as those already installed should be used. If iron and brass pipe are joined together, for instance, the iron pipe, particularly at the point where the connection has been made, may eventually be eaten away because of the galvanic action which causes the iron to dissolve over a period of time.

In most instances, rusty water can be cleared and corrosion curtailed by proper treatment of the water supply. This requires the careful introduction of suitable chemicals into the water system by specially designed chemical treating devices. Pipes that are already clogged with corrosion can be cleared so that the supply pressure and flow of water through them is made satisfactory, but this requires the services of an expert water treatment company.

Tips on Reducing Water Consumption

One minor faucet leak—producing only a thin stream (1/32 in.)—can result in a loss of up to 52,000 gallons of water a year. One leaky lavatory fixture will ordinarily waste as much as 75,000 gallons a month. Leaks in water pipes running through unexcavated sections under the floor of a motel may go on for years without being discovered so it is advisable to investigate regularly all water lines embedded in the earth. It is important that the blow-down valves of the boiler be maintained in tight condition. When leaky, these valves can waste tremendous quantities of hot water.

23 Ways to Cut Electric Bills

1. Reduce excessively high lamp wattages wherever lower wattages will furnish acceptable lighting.
2. Reduce, if possible, and then standardize the size of lamps in guest rooms. Have maids and bellmen turn off lights when not in use.
3. Consider using long life bulbs to reduce bulb cost and labor costs to change them.
4. Use fluorescent lighting whenever possible. It provides the same light as incandescent bulbs with only 1/3 of the wattage.
5. Consider use of mercury lamps. Exceptionally useful in parking lots, this type of lamp is also inexpensive.
6. Consider using time clocks for automatic switching of: signs, motors, building lights, heaters and warmers, air conditioning, water pumps, fans.
7. Experiment with alternate light switching and automatic transformer dimming to reduce the amount or intensity of nighttime corridor lighting.
8. Replace resistance dimmers with transformer type.
9. Use photoelectric cells to switch off lamps when sunlight provides adequate illumination.
10. Investigate the possibility of installing short time (twist on) timers controlling lights in store rooms and walk-in boxes or other time-use areas where lights are apt to be left on needlessly.
11. Turn off large motors when not needed: turning off one 50 horsepower motor saves as much electricity as 400 100-watt light bulbs.
12. Turn off banquet refrigerators and ice makers when not in use.
13. Turn off lights in function areas when functions are ended. Lock panels so night cleaners cannot turn on every light when only a few are required.
14. Turn off central vacuum systems after housemen have finished morning cleaning.
15. Turn off elevator motor generators when not in use. Turn off *some* automatic elevators during low traffic periods.
16. Reduce speed of motors for light service duty. If the fan or pump must run, it may be worthwhile to replace a single-speed motor with a two-speed motor. A motor operating at ½ speed consumes only ⅛ as much power as at full speed.
17. In single speed motors, reduce the drive (motor pulley) when full speed is not required. This will cut wattage consumed.
18. Enlist the aid of all staff members in turning off unused equipment and lighting.

19. Ask your power company representative to explain how low power factor can be costly. Ask him about studies to determine whether your power factor can be improved. Even when there is no power factor penalty, such improvement will be advantageous.

20. Reduce demands and sudden increases in current consumption. Ask the power company to install recording meters to help analyze your loads. If large loads can be juggled so that not all equipment is started up at once in the demand period, you should save money. Large motors should have reduced voltage starters. Demand limiting or alarm equipment is available for air conditioning or heating equipment.

21. Be sure your wiring is adequate in capacity for peak loads.

22. Check with the electric company to make certain that the service provided is the one that affords the most economical rate.

23. Check your electric bills carefully.
    a. Is rate schedule properly applied?
    b. Is arithmetic correct?
    c. Are they in line with past experience? If not, why not?
    d. Are you receiving discounts for which you are eligible?

Getting the Most From the Carpeting Dollar

It has been estimated that the American lodging industry spends about $250 million on the more than 10 million square yards of carpeting it buys annually. In addition to informed purchasing with due regard to quality and wear standards, getting the most for your carpeting dollar requires a planned maintenance program.

The first element in carpet care and maintenance is daily light vacuuming to remove loose surface dirt and to prevent soil build-up.

At this time immediate attention should be paid to spot removal to preclude permanent staining.

Third, carpets should be *thoroughly* cleaned every week with particular attention to high traffic areas and even those rooms that are infrequently used.

Seasonal cleaning means a wet shampoo at least once a year. While this can be done with the carpets in place, experts recommend that, if practical, the carpets be picked up and processed in a commercial cleaning plant.

Finally, periodic maintenance includes attention to burned or permanently stained areas of the carpeting and such mechanical problems as open seams, buckled portions, loose ends, snags, etc.. These repairs usually require the skills and equipment of an expert.

Care of Other Flooring Materials

Uncarpeted floors come in infinite variety—hardwood, many types of resilient coverings, formed-in-place and masonry. Each demands a different kind of maintenance. Detailed instructions for keeping them attractive are contained in the excellent manual,

Floors and Floor Maintenance, by Bernard Berkeley, published by the Cornell Hotel & Restaurant Administration Quarterly.

The Key to Efficient Housekeeping

An efficient housekeeping operation has the task of keeping the hotel's rooms and public areas clean and attractive. In addition to employment of the most effective cleaning materials and procedures, scientific housekeeping demands attention to *purchasing* of the most suitable linens and cleaning supplies, *decorating* for ease of maintenance and, above all, proper *organization* and *supervision*.

The housekeeping budget typically accounts for nearly 20 percent of a property's total operating expense. Since the wage cost of maids is the largest expense element in the housekeeping department, maid productivity improvement can yield substantial savings. In establishing performance standards for maids, consideration needs to be given to many factors such as the size and design of the rooms; amount, type and arrangement of furniture; type of property and operation. Productivity of maids in a commercial property understandably is generally considerably greater than in a resort, for example.

In measuring maid productivity, the vital statistic is not how many rooms a maid does in a day, but rather how many she does in an *hour*. The reason: all maids don't work an eight-hour day, and even those who do sometimes show up late or leave early, take longer lunch periods, etc..

To help maids achieve optimum productivity:

- Design guest rooms with maintenance in mind.
- Select furnishings with an eye to ease of cleaning.
- Provide suitable equipment, facilities and supplies.
- Specify performance standards.
- Staff housekeeping function adequately.
- Organize the work efficiently.
- Spell out procedures in writing.
- Provide both theoretical and practical training.
- Supply motivation and recognition.
- Give continuing and supportive supervision.
- Hire temporary personnel for peak occupancy periods.

To Buy or Not To Buy?

Whether to rent or buy linens and the pros and cons of in-house laundry vs. commercial service are subjects of continuing debate.

Since linen can be a major investment and the choice of product is not easy, smaller properties generally decide to rent linens if the rental service is both reasonable and dependable. The increasing popularity of no-iron linens and uniforms, as well, however, may swing the balance in favor of owning rather than renting.

In general, it has been found that it is cheaper to own linens and operate an on-premise laundry than to rent them. To own linens, but have them laundered commercially, usually falls between these two alternatives in cost.

A large motel in St. Petersburg, Florida, plagued with delivery problems, shortages and poor linen quality with its rental linen service, was able to save 65% on laundry bills by installing its own laundry, according to the manager.

No-Irons and Beyond

Similar savings have been reported by other properties using no-iron sheets, pillow cases, bedspreads and other linens and having staff do the work in fully automatic washers and dryers. In many cases, the existing linen storage room was large enough to accommodate the compact in-house laundry.

It is reported that many hotels and motels are cutting costs by as much as 50 percent by using no-iron linens. A case in point: a 220-room Sheraton property in Cleveland saved $15,000 the first year it had a no-iron laundry—a 50 percent saving over using an outside linen service.

No-Iron Costs: 100-125 Rooms

EQUIPMENT NEEDED:
Two 50-lb. washer-extractors with 250-lb. capacity per hour. (Average need is 220 lbs. per hour.) Two 37-by 30-inch drying tumblers, reversing cool down. One no-iron sheet folder.

CAPACITY:
Laundry can process 220 lbs. per hour or 8,800 lbs. for a 40-hour work week.

WATER CONSUMPTION PER HOUR:
Cold water: 480 gallons
Hot water: 160 gallons

SPACE REQUIRED: 20 by 20 feet

INITIAL COST:

Approximate cost of installation	$ 1,500.00
Approximate cost of equipment	11,700.00
Total equipment cost:	$13,200.00

WEEKLY OPERATING COST:

Labor: two full-time workers at $2.00 an hour	$160.00
Fringe benefits, 20% of payroll	32.00
Supply cost	37.00
Utilities	50.00
Total weekly operating cost	$279.00

Source: American Hotel & Motel Association

It may be only a matter of time until no-iron linens give way to disposables—towels, sheets and pillowcases and uniforms. Among the considerations affecting more widespread usage of disposables in the lodging industry are these:

- Acceptance by guests
- Storage and inventory requirements
- Cost
- Ready availability
- Flammability
- Disposal

Boosting Bottom Line Figures Through Profitable Hotel and Motel Food Service

In the golden age of "haute cuisine," the culinary masterpieces of chefs such as Escoffier and his disciples were only to be had in the dining rooms of the world's famous hotels. Today, with rare exceptions such as the Caribbean Room of the Pontchartrain Hotel in New Orleans, hotel fare tends to be undistinguished at best. Yet, though relatively few hotels, let alone motels, would earn plaudits for food preparation and service, most provide appetizing menus at reasonable prices.

Guests Pass Up Hotel Food

Americans like to "eat out." More than 20 percent of our food dollar is spent away from home. Are hotel and motel food facilities getting their share of this business? Unfortunately not. A study of hotel/motel guest eating patterns done by Michigan State University revealed that slightly more than half of the respondents did not eat any of their dinners and one fourth did not eat any breakfast in the lodging establishment in which they were registered. Sixty percent of the respondents ate all their breakfasts in the hotel or motel at which they were staying, while only 13 percent ate all their lunches and 20 percent ate all their dinners there. Convention guests tend to take more meals in their hotels than other travelers because of planned meal functions.

You're in the Restaurant Business

The conventional wisdom in the lodging industry is that "you can't make money on food," and it's true that in many hotels and motels food service is strictly a "loss leader" proposition provided as a convenience for guests. Yet there are hoteliers who turn a nice profit in their dining rooms and coffee shops, to say nothing of bars. Hospitality Motor Inns, it is reported, receives more revenue from its food and beverage operations than from room sales.

Among the top 20 institutions in food service sales are Howard Johnson's, Holiday Inns, Hilton, Sheraton, and Marriott. The fact that several of these chains started out as restaurant operations may be significant. Authorities suggest that, to be successful, hotels and motels should conceive of and operate their food facilities as *restaurants* competing with other area eating establishments rather than merely as adjuncts to their room business.

Trends Worth Noting

In this vein, some food service industry trends listed in a U. S. Government publication are worthy of note:
—A trend to bigness, not only for the industry overall, but for individual operations;
—A trend to chains and franchising;
—A trend to higher costs per employee and an increased need for higher productivity;
—A trend toward more training for all levels of personnel to increase productivity;
—A trend to the reduction of the number of employees needed to prepare and serve food, accompanied by increasing attention to central purchasing of food supplies, elimination of job duplication and simplification of procedures;
—A trend to maximum automation wherever appropriate—elimination or reduction of "hand" jobs, increased use of convenience foods and a "systems" approach to food preparation and service;
—A trend to limited and specialized menus;
—A trend to a marketing research approach in the design and operation of food service establishments—atmosphere, menu, hours of operation and pricing all planned to conform to pre-determined market needs and demands;
—A trend to increased demands on management and supervisory personnel in terms of responsibility for productivity, profitability and public service.

The Restaurant Market Is Segmented, Too

In planning or upgrading a hotel/motel restaurant operation, it is important to recognize the principle of market segmentation. This is a simple acknowledgement of the fact that, since all people don't want the same thing, there is no *one* best product or place to be. The secret of success, therefore, is not to search in vain for a *universally* acceptable product, but rather to concentrate on developing the best product for *each* market segment or category of people you hope to serve. Where many hotel food operations have gone wrong has been in providing only a single "dining room" which offered neither the variety and excellence of food demanded by the discriminating guest nor the inexpensive and quickly served breakfast and luncheon menus desired by such clients as neighborhood office workers and families with children. A classic example of this type of food operation was the Essex House in New York City before it was taken over by Marriott Hotels. The posh hostelry had no coffee shop and its one dining room, in which the food was well but unimaginatively prepared, had all the warmth of a glacier.

Psychology Influences Restaurant Decor

Jac Lessman, a well-known designer in the hotel/motel field, asserts that each patron has four senses that must be satisfied if his dining experience is to be enjoyable. What he *sees*, what he *smells*, what he *hears*, as well as what he *tastes*, all are important.

He points out that psychology has a great deal to do with a diner's mood and response. For example:

. . .massive decor may overwhelm a patron and make him feel uncomfortably insignificant.

. . .booths are very popular because they give patrons feelings of privacy and security—those in booths can be both part of and detached from the rest of the dining area.

. . .if lights are too bright, guests tend to feel exposed; if too low, they may feel abandoned.

Carleton Varney, Jr., one of America's leading authorities on restaurant interiors, says: "There should be a balance among what is economically prudent, functional and esthetically satisfying. A restaurant interior must 'say' something. You either re-create the feeling of the home, or you take the opposite approach—continually remind the diner that he's *not* at home, that he's enjoying an *event*."

Causes of Food Sales Decline

All restaurants and other food service establishments have the same basic operating problems—purchasing, receiving, storage, preparation and service. Deficiencies in any one of these functions can adversely affect sales. In most cases, when food sales decline, one or more of the following can be blamed:

1. *Overpricing*—particularly in comparison with competition.
2. *Poor Menu Planning*
3. *Poor Food Quality*
4. *Indifferent Service*
5. *Poor Sanitation*
6. *Unattractive, Noisy Atmosphere*
7. *Inconvenient Access*
8. *Inadequate or Ineffective Promotion*

Food and Payroll Costs Can Be Controlled

Since profitability depends on keeping sales volume up and costs down, particular attention needs to be paid to food and payroll costs in the food service operation. Inefficient purchasing, waste, overproduction, pilfering, under-pricing, improper training and inadequate supervision all contribute to high food costs. Equally, poor planning, faulty training and ineffective supervision inevitably result in high payroll costs.

Over an eight year period, a hotel complex operating a number of theme restaurants was able to cut food cost from 35.9¢ of sales to 31.4¢, a reduction of over 12 percent, using control techniques covered later in this chapter. Detailed explanations of various ways of controlling food costs, along with illustrations of many forms developed for this purpose, are to be found in *Profitable Restaurant Management* by Kenneth I. Solomon and Norman Katz, a Prentice-Hall publication.

Among the useful forms included are the following:

Daily Flash Food Cost Report—showing the aggregate of requisitions plus purchases and comparing the total cost with food sales.

Daily Summary of Food Cost—showing actual food consumption and cost by category for comparison with sales in both current and previous periods.

Monthly Consumption Report—based on physical inventories, this form discloses inventory shortages and provides cost figures for analysis and comparison.

A dramatic example of how purchasing and portion control can make or break a food operation is that of a restaurant specializing in chicken dishes. Specifications were established for purchasing chickens between 2 and 2½ pounds. On this basis, 100 pounds should yield approximately 45 chickens.

When the purveyor included 10 three pound chickens in each 100 pounds ordered, the yield was reduced to 42 chickens. The loss of three chickens per 100 pounds ordered was soon sorrowfully noticed on the bottom line!

Keep A Tight Rein on Purchasing and Receiving

Food cost control should begin with purchasing of food supplies on the basis of competitive bids to assure the lowest price for the required quality. But unless deliveries are closely monitored for both quantity and quality, food costs can still get out of hand. Among the steps that should be taken to prevent questionable practices in the supply line are these:

1. Separate the functions of purchasing and receiving.
2. Provide for written evidence that competitive bids have been sought.
3. Make sure there is a record of items ordered.
4. Insure that the person checking deliveries is reliable, knowledgeable about food quality and that he reports to the manager.
5. Check to be sure that prices quoted and prices charged do not vary.
6. Conduct frequent and unannounced spot checks of deliveries.

Holding Storage and Issuing Costs Down

The storage and issuing of food also should be carefully controlled. Following are some recommended practices:

1. Accountability should be vested in just one person. Some advise that the accounting department should have direct control of food issues.
2. Periodic inventories should be taken.
3. Occasional spot checks should be made.
4. Supplies should be issued only during established hours.
5. In issuing food, "first in-first out" should be the rule.
6. A requisition procedure should be set up so a record can be maintained of nature, quantity, pricing and date of food supplies issued.
7. To eliminate storeroom pilferage, (a) keep the storeroom door locked, (b) provide for dual control of storeroom keys in the absence of storeroom attendant, and (c) prohibit entrance into the storeroom by unauthorized persons.

How to Save Payroll Dollars

Lower staff costs in the food service operation call for a good forecasting procedure, careful scheduling and the application of realistic work standards. If payroll dollars are to be saved, it is essential that management be able to predict, with a reasonable degree of accuracy, business volume by month, week, day and meal. With this information it is then possible to staff and schedule work for optimum results.

Establish Work Standards

Work standards for the food service staff must take into consideration that the volume of work changes from one day to the next and also during different hours of the day. Serving breakfast, for instance, is less demanding and time consuming than serving dinner. A variety of other factors need also to be taken into account: type of food preparation, kitchen layout and facilities, distance from kitchen to serving area, facilities in serving area, type of service and volume of between-meal business.

Avoiding Waste

Avoidance of waste can help a great deal in keeping food costs low.
Here are some basics sometimes overlooked:

1. Proper storage to prevent spoilage
2. Utilization of left-overs
3. Control of over-production
4. Curbing of over-generous servings, including extra rolls and butter.
5. Use of standard recipes.
6. Forecasting to adjust for the impact of special days and events. Monday business, for example, is apt to be light after weekend overindulgences. Friday is still "fish day" for many people.

What a Difference an Ounce Makes!

Portion control is necessary to insure that all customers get what they are paying for. More important, it is crucial to profitability.

Assume a hotel restaurant serves 25,000 orders of roast beef a year. If the cost to serve one ounce is 15 cents, the direct loss in profit resulting from serving each customer only one extra ounce would be $3,750 a year! Put another way, if the restaurant was realizing a net profit of eight percent on sales, it would need an additional $46,875 in revenue to make up this $3,750.

Build Profits through Menu Planning

Menu studies show that 75 percent of all entree sales on luncheon and dinner menus are limited to six or seven items. When menus offer two or three times this number of entrees, the inevitable results are overproduction, waste and excessive preparation costs.

The Gallup Survey asked a representative cross-section of adult Americans about their favorite main dish when eating Sunday dinner in a restaurant. Steak, chicken, roast beef and seafood ranked in that order for the entire sample. But there were interesting variations by sex, age, income group and region.

Men were definitely beef eaters; chicken was as popular as steak with diet-conscious women; seafood was more popular than roast beef for the between 21 and 34 age group and roast beef was favored over chicken and steak by those 50 years and older. Not surprisingly, those in lower income brackets tended to pick less expensive entrees. The one place, predictably, where chicken was the top choice was the South.

A similar survey by the Gallup organization revealed that the three most popular restaurant lunches, in rank order, were (1) a hot sandwich with french fries and a hot beverage, (2) a meat, potato and vegetable dish without salad or dessert, and (3) a complete hot lunch with salad, dessert and beverage. Despite the concern about over-weight among American adults, low calorie specials were near the bottom of the list of choices.

Not only because of known food preferences, but also to reduce costs, limited menus make sense for all but the most pretentious food facilities. A limited menu provides these advantages:

1. Less inventory is required, freeing working capital and reducing handling and storage charges.
2. There is less chance of spoilage and shrinkage.
3. Since less production is required, reduction in payroll costs should be possible.

Why the Move to Convenience Foods?

A step further in expense control and assurance of uniform quality is the precooked entree. While there are those who denigrate this boon to an industry suffering from high labor costs and a scarcity of competent chefs, more and more frozen, precooked foods are being used by the nation's restaurants, hotels and motels and institutional food service operations. Apart from lower cost and reduction in waste and spoilage, the use of precooked foods allows a far greater variety of choice than all except the most innovative and skilled chefs could provide. More than 200 different frozen entrees are available from one of the leading suppliers in the field.

An example of the kind of cost savings precooked food can make possible is provided by a hospital in Chicago which, in changing over to convenience foods, was able to realize a decrease in waste from 25 percent to two percent, a reduction in kitchen staff from 17 to four and a substantial saving in space.

According to Marshall Warfel, formerly Sheraton's vice president of food and beverage operations, a 50 percent improvement in that chain's food profits over a six year period was brought about by better management, more effective buying procedures, improved staff cooperation, better pricing, study of consumer preferences, use of staffing guides and bar charts and increased utilization of convenience foods.

As much as one-fourth of foods served by Sheraton properties, Warfel says, are convenience foods ranging from appetizers and soups through desserts. Warfel's prediction is that within the very near future more than 25 percent of hotels and restaurants now existing will be using convenience foods exclusively.

A Viable Alternative—"Ready Foods"

A variation of the convenience food concept under which precooked foods are purchased from outside suppliers is the "Ready Foods" system developed by Cornell University's School of Hotel Administration. Cornell defines it as "the application of mass production to an a la carte food service with prepared-to-order foods." The "Ready Foods" system calls for entrees, basic sauces, soups, vegetables and desserts to be prepared, packaged, frozen, stored and served, all on the same premises. Foods are prepared in large quantities (four to six weeks' supply) at one time, usually during slack periods for cooks. After preparation and cooking, the food is packaged in one or two portion plastic packages which are kept in frozen inventory until ordered by the guest when they are heated in boiling water, deep fat or micro-wave ovens.

Among the advantages cited for the Cornell "Ready Foods" system are these:

1. It employs mass production techniques, thus saving labor and economizing on raw materials.
2. Once the items are prepared under the supervision of a qualified chef, unskilled workers can reheat the frozen dishes for serving.
3. Portion control is facilitated.
4. Recipes can be exclusive.
5. Uniformity of quality is enhanced and additives are not required.
6. "Ready Foods" may be produced at savings of up to one third of the cost of purchasing comparable frozen items from outside sources.
7. Shortages are minimized and leftovers practically eliminated since all food prepared is sold.

Showmanship Is Important

Given good quality food, well prepared, what can either make or ruin a meal is the atmosphere in which it is served, the *presentation.* Merchandising the meal experience deserves to be high on the priority list of innkeepers who wish to run a profitable and pleasurable food service operation.

J. B. Temple, formerly President, Lodging Division, Holiday Inns of America, Inc., recognizes this fact when he says, "Many products are basically identical except for perhaps a five percent difference, and it is this difference that is advertised and makes a product sell better than another."

Referring specifically to the food service operation in a hotel or motel, Temple makes these observations:

"Likewise in the super-restaurant at breakfast time, there is a cart showing the fresh fruit offerings so the waitress does not have to tell about them (or not tell, as is the usual fashion). This same cart is used for salad displays at lunchtime, during the summer, or steaks and seafood cocktails at night.

"A buffet can be prepared so that it is colorful, with interesting, attractively displayed food, unusual containers, decent serving spoons, and accent lighting. Colorful cloth mats can be used at lunchtime, or at dinner, if an informal yet nice appearance is desired. Candles can be used for the evening meal, and the lights dimmed. For many years I have been trying to get candles used for all banquets, with lights dimmed. This makes the banquet a party instead of a stark, brightly lighted factory type meal. When I used to be a banquet manager, I always had a spotlight at the head table, with perhaps some candelabra and flowers, with the rest of the room dimmed, with a simple candle in a simple glass candleholder on each table, and a little greenery added.

"So many of our innkeepers and supervisors do not seem to realize that we are in the show business, or theater business. People take a trip, visit our inns, take a drink, or eat a meal with us hopefully to get a pleasant and exciting psychological experience. Let's give them what they want, and we'll all make more money, achieve satisfaction, and have fun. That is the reason we try to have music, and good lighting, and attractive uniforms. They really are costumes, you know, just as in a theater. The Great Sign and its changeable letters is our theater marquee, and the innkeeper is the ringmaster for what can be 'the greatest show on earth.'"

A Look into the Crystal Ball

That increasing attention will be paid by innkeepers to their food and beverage operations in the future is predicted by Stephen Brener, Senior Vice President, Helmsley-Spear, Inc., a hospitality industry consultant with impressive credentials. "The excuse of a typical hotel man; that he is not a restaurant man or that he's not in the food business, is nonsense," says Brener. "Hotels must be able to make money on their food operations, like Howard Johnson's and other chains are now doing. The big change in the 70's will be the attempt of hostelries to show a profit on their food operations. And the industry has to overcome a long-standing image held by the American public that, when traveling, they should avoid hotel restaurants and coffee shops. The public has been taught not to eat in hotels."

What are some of the directions this increased attention to hotel/motel dining facilities might take? A study of motivational research offers these clues:

1. The future of the classic expensive restaurant seems limited. No longer the status symbol it once was, it also is not congruent with today's life style which emphasizes informality and calorie consciousness.

2. Fast food operations are going to have to upgrade their offerings to please more sophisticated and more affluent customers who seek more varied menus and higher quality food.

3. Informal food facilities featuring value and "serve yourself" salad sections are making inroads on traditional white napery eating places.

4. The popularity of outdoor cooking offers interesting possibilities for motels with suitable space as well as resort properties.

5. Visual merchandising of food preparation and service can promote appetite appeal. The chef at the out-front carving board is an example of this.

6. The menu itself can be made into a merchandising tool. More colorful and descriptive copy could be used. Photos could be used more effectively to illustrate types of food and size of portions. "Visible" menus featuring facsimiles of actual servings on display, as many Japanese restaurants do, are another possible device to merchandise food.

If You Decide to Lease Your Restaurant . . .

For various reasons, some innkeepers may prefer to lease out their restaurant and/or coffee shop rather than operate these facilities themselves. Often this can work out to be quite a profitable arrangement for the innkeeper which allows him to provide needed food facilities for guests without the admitted "headaches" of running them. Since the quality of food served, prices and service standards will reflect on the hotel or motel itself, however, extreme care should be taken in choosing the restaurateur to whom the space will be leased.

An American Hotel & Motel Association Operations Bulletin offers this advice:

1. Make a survey, including a rental market appraisal, to determine which type of rental agreement will be of greatest benefit to the landlord.
2. Determine basis for computing rental:
   (a) *Fixed rental:* uniform payments throughout term of lease.
   (b) *Graduated lease:* rent graded upward as lease matures.
   (c) *Percentage lease:* rent paid according to:
      1. fixed or sliding percentage of sales or profit,
      2. a minimum fixed rental or a percentage of sales or profit, whichever is greater,

3. a minimum fixed sum plus a percentage of sales or profit.

(d) *Reappraised rental value lease:*

After a short term during which rent is fixed, it is increased or decreased according to a reappraisal of the value of the space occupied or gross sales.

Usually, the most satisfactory arrangement is one giving the landlord a minimum rental plus a percentage of gross sales.

3. Spell out in the lease who pays for maintenance and other charges. If an adequate return on value of the space is to be earned, the tenant should pay for—

a. Installation and upkeep of furnishings, fixtures and equipment.

b. Silver, glass, china, kitchen utensils and all movable items.

c. Utilities

d. Cleaning, repairing and maintaining the leased space.

4. Require that the tenant provide certain services for the hotel or motel such as room service, meals for staff, banquet and other catering service, fixed price food service if the property offers American or Modified American plans.

5. Avoid a long-term lease—a 10-year term usually works out best from the landlord's point of view.

6. If possible, do not include a renewal option clause in the lease.

7. Be sure the lease retains for the landlord the right to approve any sublease or assignment of the original lease and, if possible, that it includes a cancellation clause favoring the landlord.

Besides the rental arrangement, a lease should include:

1. detailed description of the premises
2. plans of the space
3. clauses covering the services and facilities that the landlord is supplying
4. list of duties and responsibilities of the tenant
5. percentage of real estate taxes tenant is to pay
6. how utility charges are to be handled
7. water and sewerage cost allocation
8. control of access from and to space
9. insurance requirements—fire, liability, etc.
10. provisions covering partial and complete loss via condemnation or fire
11. agreement on hours and days of operation
12. determination of the quality of product
13. range of retail price of items to be sold
14. disposition of receipts from vending, counter and other sales.

7

Modern Hotel and
Motel Sales and Promotion:
Tools and Techniques

It is almost axiomatic that every marketing man has his own favorite definition of "marketing." Often the experts become so enamored of semantic hair-splitting that they lose sight of the simple fact that, in its most basic and honest form, marketing is nothing more than "pleasing people at a profit."

A little more altruistic, yet no less apt definition is the one advanced by Kotler and Levy, "sensitively serving and satisfying human needs."[1]

Marketing is the *total* process by which goods and services are designed, presented, merchandised and delivered to the ultimate consumer. At the same time, it is the heart of a dynamic, free society. In its relentless searching to fulfill people's wants and needs on a voluntary free choice basis, it directs purposeful change. It starts and progresses the process whereby human goals are enlarged in the very act of their being served.

Of one thing, there is no doubt: marketing is the key to success in the lodging industry as in any other business. Management consultant Peter Drucker asserts that a business has only two basic functions: marketing and innovation. He supports the distinction that "selling focuses on the needs of the seller, while marketing focuses on the needs of the buyer."

The one thing marketing is not—and no less an authority than C. DeWitt Coffman, former President of Treadway Inns and Resorts, preaches this gospel—is just "a fancy or postgraduate form of selling." Coffman asserts there are really six components to marketing for the hospitality industry: people, product, package, price, promotion, and performance.

---

[1] Philip Kotler and Sidney Levy, "Broadening the Concept of Marketing," *Journal of Marketing*, Vol. 33 (January, 1969), p. 15.

Components of an Integrated Marketing System

In developing a marketing plan for an operating facility or one still on the drawing board, each of these elements must be considered as part an integrated system.

People: Who are the present or potential customers; where are they; what are their needs, desires and constraints?

Product: What are the existing or planned facilities and services; how closely do they match or can they be made to correspond with what guests want?

Price: The quid pro quo which must take into consideration the innkeeper's need to operate at a profit while offering a product which is competitive not only with other comparable lodging facilities, but which can compete with other products seeking the consumer dollar—vacations abroad, second homes, camping, even jewelry and furs.

Promotion: Utilization of all appropriate communication media and merchandising tools to attract the attention of the prospect, to persuade him that the product and price are right *for him* and then to close the sale.

Performance: Living up to what has been promised in every respect in order to maximize the guests's length of stay and amount of spending and so he becomes an ambassador of good will for the property as well as a repeat customer himself.

What Is a Market?

The word "market" can be used in many ways. Among them are these:

1. The location where a sale takes place.
2. The geographical area where a particular supply of goods is usually sold, or from which a particular supply is procured.
3. The specific institutions or channels through which the marketing process takes place.
4. The complex set of forces that causes a particular price to be paid for some amount of goods and/or services.

What Is a Lodging Market?

The "market" for hotel/motel facilities and services consists of all of those people and organizations that *realistically* might constitute buyers.

Within this complex of potential customers there are a number of discrete groups called "market segments." Each may have its own unique characteristics, needs and demands. The lodging market can be segmented according to many measures, but leading the list would have to be these:

Age	Purpose of travel
Sex	Income

Size of Family   Occupation

Education   Mode of travel

While for purposes of analysis it is useful to break out or segment markets in this fashion, one should not lose sight of the fact that markets are constantly shifting and changing in complexion. Therefore, while ideally the most concentrated marketing effort should be bestowed on the most promising segment, consideration should also be given to appealing to and serving presently marginal segments.

An example of this approach is the venerable Plaza Hotel in New York City which, while still catering to the dowager and diplomat trade, added an ice cream soda bar and other amenities to attract a younger and more feisty clientele.

On the other hand, as the sales manager of the *New Yorker* magazine told a group of leading lodging industry executives, "You don't hire the finest French Chef and then pack in the girls' roller skating team from Dubuque."

The point is, you identify and direct the big guns of your marketing arsenal at your primary market while, at the same time, taking advantage of "targets of opportunity" in other less productive segments.

Examples abound of how astute market research helped fill rooms that otherwise would be becoming musty and dusty.

One New York City chain, for instance, found that, for some inexplicable reason, its properties had a particular appeal for New Englanders. Armed with this intelligence, it mounted an advertising campaign that had proper Bostonians descending upon its mid-town hotels in droves.

Integrating Elements of Marketing

Market research must undergird any effective marketing strategy and program. Data are available both from secondary and primary sources. Secondary sources include statistics available from the U.S. Department of Commerce, the business and trade press, trade associations, Chambers of Commerce, university research, etc.. Primary sources include market studies by the hotel/motel organization, observation and direct inquiry by staff of guests.

Unfortunately, little, if any, progress in the market research area has been made by the lodging industry since Curt Strand, President, Hilton International Company, made the following statement in 1971: "In the field of market research, our industry couldn't possibly do less than it has done in the past—it has almost always followed the trends without anticipating them."

Yet, while market research can be very complex and esoteric, in the main it involves compilation and interpretation of readily available basic market data.

One of the most effective tools available to every innkeeper is the guest questionnaire. In years gone by, hotels used to maintain detailed guest histories listing room and other preferences of guests, frequency and timing of visits and a host of other facts useful in knowing and selling the market. Discarded by most properties as too time-consuming to maintain, and poorly followed up on where they still are in use, guest histories can be a useful research tool.

The great advantage of "Guest History" records, according to John Patafio, Sr., a direct mail expert, is that in no other way can you classify "types", "interests", etc., and so make your direct mail matter have all the attributes of a straight personally written letter, and at the same time make your appeal to a KNOWN interest or preference of that guest.

For example, those guests who have shown preferences for boxing and the cocktail lounge can be sorted out and addressed a letter which bears down on those particular items. Those who enjoyed the theatres, or who were baseball fans, or who went in for football, can be appealed to in the same way.

Most of the information on a guest history card can be noted by simply checking the item. Your room clerk can do that, if the cards are stacked near by.

NAME ______________________
LAST NAME FIRST NAME

ADDRESS:
HOME: ______________________
BUSINESS: ______________________
SUMMER: ______________________
WINTER ______________________

Jan.	Feb.	Mar	Apr.	May	Jun	July	Aug	Sept	Oct.	Nov	Dec.

CREDIT ______________

SPECIAL EVENTS	ACTIVITIES			PATRONAGE	EXTRA SERVICES
Birthday: ______	☐ Skiing	☐ Hiking	☐ Dancing	☐ Dining Room	
Wedding Anniversary: ______	☐ Tennis	☐ Bathing	☐ Concert	☐ Cocktail Lounge	COMPLAINTS
Religion: ______	☐ Golf	☐ Fishing	☐ Lectures	☐ Retiring	
Approx. Age: ______	☐ Saddle Horse	☐ Picnics		☐ Active	

Hotel	Date Arrival	Date Departure	Room No.	Number of People	Rate	Revenue	Origin Record	Solicitation Record	REMARKS

Created by Ambassador Mail Advertising Co., 2050 Bellmore Avenue, Bellmore, L. I., N. Y.

Figure 7-1

Hotel Guest History Card

MONTH OF THE YEAR. By checking the month of arrival, you can build up repeat business by sending letters out a month or so in advance of previous arrival date.

NAME AND ADDRESS. Permanent home address is important, but in many cases a letter might better be sent to business address.

CREDIT AND ACCOUNT NO. Needs no elaboration.

SPECIAL EVENTS. It is surprising how much "come-hither" there is in sending a letter relative to an anniversary, suggesting a celebration by taking a trip to the hotel.

SPORTS. By knowing what sports your guests are interested in, you can write letters at appropriate times to induce a trip to your hotel.

PATRONAGE. This will give valuable information as to HOW desirable the guest is—if he is a good spender.

EXTRA SERVICES. If a guest requires extra services of any kind, a memo in this column will help a lot to guide you the following year.

COMPLAINTS. It is often found that a perfectly adjusted "complaint" will still rankle in a guest's mind after leaving the hotel. It often saves loss of patronage if you REMEMBER, and forestall any repetition of the situation.

RESERVATION. Knowing who actually made the reservation may help in going after the one who does the deciding.

REVENUE. Knowing the total revenue from each guest eliminates guess-work as to desirability of keeping after a particular individual as a good customer.

ORIGIN RECORD. Note if recommended by some other guest (who should be noted), or from letter sent out (and what prospect list), or if guest saw your advertisement in a paper, on a road sign, or other means of promotion.

SOLICITATION RECORD. Dates and type of solicitation should be recorded, and the number of follow-ups required. Letters sent out should be KEPT in a file, and referred to by number in this column.

Figure 7-2

ARCHRIS Hotel Corp. uses attractive and easy to fill out "comment cards" to get guests' reactions to facilities and services. Code enables management to determine which of its properties the comment came from.

REMARKS. Left for notation of anything overlooked, such as if guest is undesirable and why, or highly desirable.

Supplementing the data to be found on registration cards, questionnaires can be used to determine guest demographics such as age, income and occupation as well as psychographics—purpose of travel, life style and attitudinal measures. Direct questions can also elicit evaluations of the property's facilities and services. The latter is often accomplished by having the questionnaire placed in the guest rooms.

The purpose of all this probing, of course, is to establish a "guest profile"—*who* they are, *where* they come from, *how, why, when.*

Additional data of value in market planning can come from the accounting operation—daily reports on occupancy, rates, food covers, average checks, average length of stay, etc..

Research Helps Discover Virgin Markets

Hopefully, an objective analysis of the market will reveal a great deal of information about your present guest profile. With luck, you might even be able to isolate some new or virgin markets that your property could serve.

Motels on a major artery that had been by-passed by an interstate highway found, for example, that properly cultivated local business could more than take up the slack caused by lost transient trade.

What Guest Surveys Reveal

It is a truism that the key to success in business is pleasing people. J. W. Keener, former President of B. F. Goodrich Co., stated this dramatically when he said: "Everything starts with the needs and the wants of the ultimate customer. The nature of the product—its specifications—its style—its color—its size—its quality—its price—all must be suited to what the ultimate customer thinks he needs and wants."

What, in general, *do* guests want?

In a survey done by the Cornell University School of Hotel Administration, the following ranked near the top.

- free parking
- air conditioning
- soundproof walls
- room temperature control
- closet space for two people with clothes hangers
- cake soap
- coffee shop in the building
- In short, *comfort* and *convenience.*

Obviously there were variations in responses by occupation, mode of travel, income,

MAY WE ASK YOU TO TAKE A MOMENT TO GIVE US YOUR OPINION OF OUR SERVICES AND FACILITIES. YOUR COMMENTS WILL BE VERY MUCH APPRECIATED AND WILL BE COMPLETELY CONFIDENTIAL.

1. WAS YOUR RESERVATION HANDLED PROMPTLY AND COURTEOUSLY?

   Yes   No   Comment: _____
   □   □   _____

2. WAS YOUR RESERVATION ACCURATE AS YOU REQUESTED IT?

   Yes   No   Comment: _____
   □   □   _____

3. WAS THE SERVICE YOU RECEIVED AT THE REGISTRATION DESK PROMPT, FRIENDLY AND COURTEOUS?

   Yes   No   Comment: _____
   □   □   _____

4. WAS YOUR ROOM CLEAN, PLEASANT AND COMFORTABLE?

   Yes   No   Comment: _____
   □   □   _____

5. WE WOULD WELCOME ANY COMMENTS ON OUR RESTAURANTS OR COCKTAIL LOUNGES.

   Peacock Alley _____

   Bull and Bear _____

   Empire Room _____

   Oscar's _____

   Sir Harry's _____

6. DID YOU RECEIVE FRIENDLY AND COURTEOUS SERVICE FROM THE

	Yes	No		Yes	No
Doorman	□	□	Credit Office	□	□
Bellman	□	□	Room Service (phone)	□	□
Maid	□	□	Room Service (Waiter)	□	□
Telephone Operator	□	□	Valet Service	□	□
Mail and Message Desk	□	□	Laundry Service	□	□
Cashier	□	□	Assistant Manager	□	□

   Comment: _____
   _____

7. DID YOU USE OUR GARAGE? WAS IT SATISFACTORY?

   Yes   No   Comment: _____
   □   □   _____

8. DO YOU ALWAYS STAY AT THE WALDORF-ASTORIA WHEN YOU VISIT NEW YORK? IF NOT, WHAT CAN WE DO SO THAT YOU WILL WANT TO STAY HERE ALL THE TIME?

   Yes   No   Comment: _____
   □   □   _____

9. AS A FINAL THOUGHT, COULD WE IMPROVE OUR SERVICES OR FACILITIES TO BETTER SUIT YOUR NEEDS AND DESIRES AS A GUEST?

   Comment: _____
   _____
   _____

Optional

Name _____

Business Address _____
or
Home Address _____

City _____ State _____ Zip Code _____

Date of Visit _____ Room Number _____

Figure 7-3

At New York City's prestigious Waldorf-Astoria Hotel, a somewhat more detailed guest questionnaire is left in guest rooms. A high proportion of guests fill in such questionnaires with thoughtful and often helpful suggestions for improving services and/or facilities.

purpose of travel, sex, age, frequency of travel and personal travel as against travel on expense account.

Another survey, this one by Gallup, found that patrons of the best known chain hotels and motels in the U.S. placed cleanliness, reasonable prices and comfort at the top of their lists. Near the bottom was "swimming pool." In this study, too, there were demographically influenced variations, but they were not substantial.

Quit Chasing Existing Business and Start Tapping New Markets

Although long-term trends such as increasing affluence, better education, earlier retirement, etc. can be counted on to create a broader market overall for the lodging industry, there are numerous opportunities today where creative selling can generate substantial amounts of new business.

More than 60 percent of trips taken by the U.S. population are primarily for pleasure, but only about 31 percent of hotel/motel users are pleasure travelers. The majority of pleasure travelers still stay with friends or relatives or camp out.

Sources of New Business

1. *Non-business travelers.* While the business traveler may be the most important single source of revenue for some properties, young people, youthful families and the elderly constitute a numerically far greater market.

2. *Women.* Young women rate travel high, can afford it. Mature women have money, will travel. More attention needs to be paid to providing and promoting facilities and activities of particular appeal to females. Wives of business travelers represent a largely untapped source of additional business which can be cultivated by means of special rates or other inducements for wives accompanying their husbands on business trips or to conventions. "Lady Hilton" rooms planned with women's needs and desires in mind are a step in this direction.

3. *The Mass Market.* More than 80 percent of Americans with no more than high school education—clerks, secretaries, blue collar workers—are looking to travel as an escape and status symbol. This is the group from which most pleasure travelers of the future will come. Even those in low income brackets—one third of all U.S. families—can be attracted by economy accommodations such as "Motel 6" on the West Coast and many similar chains in the East and South. Family plans, off-season rates and similar merchandising approaches can be effective.

4. *Special Interest Groups.* Even though often relatively small, a surprisingly good source of business can be affinity groups such as senior citizens clubs, professional groups, hobbyists and travel clubs.

One Marriott Hotel general manager increased weekend occupancy from 30 percent to 86 percent by seeking out the business of government employees, military personnel and ethnic groups.

Figure 7-4

Award winning ad prepared by VANSANT-DUGDALE, Baltimore, MD, to attract military personnel to Crystal City Marriott Hotel.

5. *Corporate Meetings* . . . and, depending on size of property and location, convention and incentive travel business.

Well over 300,000 corporate meetings, seminars, etc. are held every year ranging from large-scale annual shareholder meetings to small training sessions. A new specialization—corporate meeting planner—is growing rapidly and a high degree of professionalism is being developed in this area.

Success in reaching this market hinges on having the right facilities and getting to the decision-makers. Since those who plan corporate meetings may hold any of a number of titles, the most direct way to get your story across to them is through one of the several excellent trade publications covering this field.

6. *The Black Travel Market.* Nearly 12 percent of all Americans—25 million people—are black. With their income rising, along with their educational level, U. S. blacks constitute a near $40 billion market for goods and services. They spend, according to *Travel Weekly*, nearly 30 percent of their income on travel. D. Parke Gibson, Negro marketing consultant, suggests a three-part formula for developing additional Negro business:

a. *Recognize* the Negro market.
b. Help the Negro market to *identify* as a market.
c. *Invite* the Negro market by making it clear its business is welcomed and desired.

7. *The Non-Customer.* Over and above the major special markets indicated above, there is the non-customer. He represents (a) the 50 percent of the U. S. population who have *never* stayed overnight in a hotel or motel, (b) the 52 percent of the population who have *never* been more than 200 miles from home, and (c) the 45 percent of the population who *do not* go away on vacation.

One or more of the following describes the non-customer:

1. He does not know about your product.
2. He cannot find your product.
3. He does not need your product.
4. He does not understand what your product can do for him.
5. He has had trouble with your product.
6. He does not believe your product offers competitive value.
7. He prefers a competitive product.
8. He does not think he will get good service.
9. He does not know or trust your name.

These clues point the way to finding out in what ways your property might be deficient in what it provides, what it does and what it fails to do. Turned around, they can form the basis for a positive and aggressive marketing effort that can produce spectacular results.

The Third Element in the Marketing Mix

At this point, two of the three elements of the marketing plan should be in place:

1. *The Customer/Prospect Mix*—who are present customers and who are desired as customers?
2. *The Services Mix*—what needs and wants of each group are now being met and which should be met in the future?

The third element, the *Promotion Mix*, deals with assessing how demand is being cultivated and sustained, as well as how it *should be*. Included in the Promotion Mix are advertising, promotion, merchandising, personal selling, etc..

The following comprehensive, but not definitive, check list, prepared by Koehl, Landis & Landan, Inc., a New York advertising agency with many hotel/motel clients, should serve as a guide in improving the extent and the impact of your property's advertising-promotion campaign.

Newspaper Advertising	Soap Wrappers	Preparation of
Local	Laundry & Valet Promotion	Verbal Sales
National	Lobby Posters	Messages For

Magazine Advertising
Outdoor Advertising
  Highway
  Railroad
  Station Poster
Radio
Television
Direct Mail
Car Cards
Trade Papers
Rack Folders
Menus
Beverage Lists
Table "Tent" Cards
Menu Flyers
Service Directories
Stationery
Post Cards
Match Books
Convention Signs &
  Display Material
All-inclusive "Package"
  Promotions
Banquet & Convention
  Brochures
Novelties
Trade-marks & Emblems
  for Printed Material,
  Uniforms, Service
  Plates, Linens, etc.
Slogans
Coordination of Color
  & Design
Special Promotions
  Fashion Shows
  Holiday Parties, etc.

Elevator Cards
"Do Not Disturb" Cards
"Maid" Cards
Registration Cards
Reservation Forms
Business Cards
Sales Letters
Key Tag Designs
Letter Stickers
Cocktail Napkins
Cocktail Coasters
Highball Stirrers
Shipping Labels
Baggage Stickers & Tags
Shoe Cloths
Wash Cloths
Razor Blade Cloths
Laundry Bags
Entertainment Promotion
Special Material for
  Fire Prevention,
  Water Conservation, etc.
Employees Operating
  Manuals
Rate Sheets
Daily Function Boards
Desk Calendars
Photography
  Black & White
  Color
Interior Promotion for
  Concessionaires

Personnel (Ele-
  vator Operators,
  Bellmen, Waiters,
  Telephone Opera-
  tors, etc.)
Birthday Cards
Christmas Cards
Credit Cards
Travel Agency
  Promotional Mat'l.
Advertising Display
  Material for Travel
  Agents, Gasoline
  Stations, etc.
Production of Sound
  Motion Pictures
Roof Signs
Exterior Displays
Advertising Valances
  for Marquees
Naming New Rooms &
  Restaurants
Design & Preperation
  of Telephone Book
  Covers
Timetable Advertising
Speeches by Execu-
  tives, Articles,
  etc.
Labels for Private
  Bottling
Remembrance Adver-
  tising
Publicity

Formula for Sales Success

"Get the confidence of the public and you have no difficulty in getting their patronage. Inspire your whole force with the right spirit of service; encourage every sign of the true spirit. So display and advertise wares that customers shall buy with understanding. Treat them as guests when they come and when they go, whether or not they buy. Give them all that can be given fairly, on the principle that to him that giveth shall be given. Remember always that the recollection of quality remains long after the price is forgotten."—Retailing "great" H. Gordon Selfridge.

Concentrate Your Efforts for Dramatic Results

In highly competitive businesses such as the innkeeping business, growth in profits will not result from merely raising prices because by so doing the market is narrowed. Profit growth must come from reduced costs or increased sales.

As management consultant Peter Drucker has observed: "In business as in all of life, a small number of events account for most of the obtainable results.

"Ten items in a product line of 1,000 usually produce three quarters of the sales; a handful of customers, among many thousands, usually account for the bulk of the orders."

The suggestions that follow are intended to help the reader get the most efficient results from his advertising-promotion-sales dollar.

1. Your best bet is to cultivate those who have been customers in the past.
2. "Use a rifle instead of a shotgun." Concentrate on a few effective marketing tools and use them well rather than try to do everything at once.
3. Stick with the tried and true. If newspaper advertising has given good results previously, don't cut back on it to try some new, unproven gimmick.
4. Talk the language of the customer. Use those media which get through to him and emphasize the appeals that are most meaningful to him.

How to Get the Most Out of Your Advertising

There are many good reasons for employing a competent advertising agency to help in evaluating the market, selecting media and preparing and placing ads. But, even if you have a highly-rated ad agency, it doesn't hurt to "keep them honest" by making sure these rules are observed:

1. *Have an advertising plan*—not advertising plans. The overall marketing strategy should dictate the goals and the advertising plan should chart a path to their attainment.
2. *Be flexible.* Don't be blinded to unusual opportunities simply because they weren't part of your plan.
3. *Synergize!* Take advantage of the help offered by other companies. Tie in, directly or indirectly, with their ads and promotions.
4. *Simplify!* Don't try to accomplish too much, sell too much, or get too complicated in a single ad. The object is to inform and persuade, not confuse.
5. *Don't Go Off the Deep End*—Exaggeration and overselling make poor advertising and unhappy customers.
6. *Be Customer Oriented*—Make sure your ads promise benefits to the customer and proof that the facilities and services will be as promised. Use examples.
7. *Test the Results.* Ask guests if they have seen your advertisements, what they think of them, whether they were influenced by the ads in making their "buying" decision.

Planning Your Advertising Budget

On the average, hotels/motels spend about five per cent of room sales income on advertising and sales promotion. Transient hotels and motels, as might be expected, spend less than half the amount year-round resorts do. The breakdown of how this money is spent depends on a number of factors such as size and age of the property, location and identified market.

A typical breakdown of media utilized, expressed as ratios to room sales:

Printed materials	.5%
Franchise fee	.7%
Signs	.8%
Radio & TV	1.1%
Newspapers and magazines	1.0%
Miscellaneous	1.7%
Total	5.8%

A budget (exclusive of agency fees) for a resort motor hotel with room sales of $500,000 might look something like this:

Printed Materials (rack brochure, weekend package folder, convention kit)	$ 9,000
Outdoor Advertising	3,000
Newspaper Advertising	5,000
Magazine and Directory Advertising	5,000
Direct Mail Advertising	2,500
Publicity, including Photography	1,500
Business Promotion	1,000
Radio	1,500
Reserve	1,500
(6% of room sales)	$30,000

Following are suggestions on "getting more bang for the buck" from a variety of advertising and promotional media.

Direct Mail

About $2.5 billion are spent annually on direct mail advertising in the U.S., making it second only to newspapers as an advertising medium. It is the most widely used promotional tool employed by the lodging industry because of these advantages:

A. *Selectivity.* You pick the people you want your message to reach.
B. *Timing.* You can choose when your message will be received.
C. *Flexibility.* You can control the size, shape and format of the material.
D. *Cost Efficiency.* While it may be the most expensive medium in terms of what it costs to reach an individual prospect, it is probably the least expensive in terms of reaching a selected group.
E. *Versatility.* It can be used for a wide variety of purposes.

A successful direct mail campaign hinges on:

A. An accurate and carefully selected list of names.
B. A well written, attractively produced letter with a compelling sales message.

Direct mail these days goes far beyond the literate and persuasive sales letter or attractive folder. Pop-up figures or devices, packaged materials and die cut brochures are just a few of the attention-getting materials creative promotional minds are developing.

To improve penetration of the Group and Business Meeting market for Holiday Inns, CURTIN & PEASE of Chicago created a series of four mailings. The key to the success of the campaign was a prior analysis of the market conducted via a mail survey. Those who responded in a positive manner were placed on the mailing list to receive the subsequent three mailings in the campaign.

In developing mailing lists, these rules should be observed.

1. *Draw up detailed specifications.* Spell out the income brackets, places of residence, occupations, etc. of those you want to reach. A study of guest profiles, as well as your current marketing plan, can establish these parameters. The purpose for which a list is to be used should be kept in mind since a list of names to cultivate social events business would obviously be vastly different than one whose object was to bring in business meetings. Also, in the interest of economy, be realistic. Take into consideration that, for many reasons, not all names in a given category may be likely prospects.

2. *Insist on Currency.* In a highly mobile society, residences and business affiliations change frequently. By all means, be sure your lists are compiled from the most current sources and that they are kept up-to-date.

You can compile your own lists from your files and utilizing sources such as local telephone and city directories, organization membership lists, etc.. *The Guide to American Directories* lists nearly 3,500 directories which can be used to compile mailing lists. Or mailing lists to meet your requirements can be purchased from professional mailing list firms.

There is real money to be saved by more effective use of direct mail. These tips can help increase the efficiency of your direct mail advertising:

A. Use lightweight paper. There is available 35 lb. stock so light that a 12-page folder with pages 7½ by 8½ inches in size can be mailed with a two-page letter and a regular reply card and still not exceed one ounce.

B. Reduce the page size and number of pages in folders and brochures.

C. Substitute a memo or note for a standard letter.

D. Say more with fewer words. Use charts, fact sheets, illustrations in place of straight narration.

E. Opt in favor of more frequent lightweight mailings rather than a one-shot "blockbuster." They can end up costing less and being many times more effective.

F. Time mailings for maximum impact. It's a lot more difficult to sell a ski resort in April than in February.

G. Keep the list lean. Marginal prospects can be weeded out. Check for duplications.

H. Weigh carefully whether the extra cost of postage-paid reply cards and envelopes is justified by returns.

we'll help you find the right slot

A lot of wheels spin into motion when the handle on a slot machine is pulled. Round-and-round the wheels spin and where they'll stop . . . no one knows. Three cherries, three oranges, two of a kind or maybe the jackpot . . . the odds are that the slot machine will be the winner . . . Except this one. Note the winning combination (shown in the windows) on the enclosed reply card and your name will be entered in a drawing for a trip for two to the Holiday Inn in Curacao, Netherlands Antilles (Caribbean).

When our Group and Business Meeting Office helps you find the right slot for your meetings, you can be sure you have a winner everytime. Whatever the size of the meetings, the locations, the complexity of the plans, Holiday Inns can help you "hit the jackpot."

You don't even have to put a dime in the slot. Our Group and Business Meeting Offices have numbers you can call collect at anytime. And *one* call does it all . . . from arranging locations, times, rooms, transportation, food, audio/visual and other meeting equipment, entertainment and all of the little extras you would expect from "the most accommodating people in the world."

There are 1450 Holiday Inns around the world. One or more offers the exact facilities and location you want. Just phone collect the office nearest you for complete details—

Chicago 312/663-0515   Salt Lake City 801/521-2570
Memphis 901/362-4638   Toronto 416/363-8086
New York 212/736-3495

—and mention the slot machine winning combination to enter your name in the drawing (a week for two including transportation, breakfasts and dinners and an exciting view of the Caribbean from your room at the Holiday Inn, Curacao—Netherlands Antilles). Or, check the enclosed card.

Holiday Inns INC 3796 LAMAR AVENUE MEMPHIS, TENNESSEE 38118 U.S.A. 901/362-4201

Figure 7-5

Folder containing a pop-up slot machine when opened promises that Holiday Inns will help business meeting planners "find the right slot."

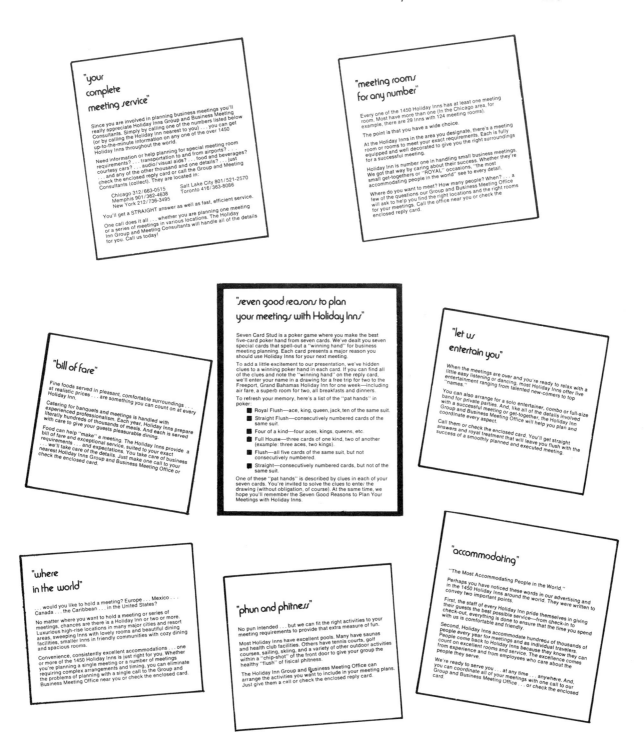

Based on the theme of "taking the gamble out of business meeting planning," Holiday Inn's direct mail campaign, an HSMA award winner, sent deck of cards to a selected list of key contacts. Cards illustrated items such as meeting rooms, accommodations and food on the face and supported photos with back-up copy on reverse side.

Figure 7-6

To get *results* from your direct mail:

1. Get to the point at the outset. Instead of beating around the bush, tell the reader in the beginning of your letter or folder what's new or different about your property.
2. Answer the question, "What's in it for me?" Emphasize the benefits to the reader.
3. Write simply. Keep sentences and paragraphs short. Avoid flossy language.
4. Be specific. Give examples and use illustrations to achieve believability.
5. Ask for the order. Make it easy for the prospect to reply by enclosing an envelope or business reply card.

The direct mail campaign created by GARDNER, STEIN and FRANK, Inc. of Chicago for the MGM Grand Hotel in Las Vegas was the "Best in Show" winner in a recent Hotel Sales Management Association advertising award contest. One piece was a colorful "mod" folder.

The grand, golden days of Hollywood have returned. To Las Vegas. To the MGM Grand Hotel. A $100 million dollar fantasy. A production bigger and more breathtaking than anything Cecil B. DeMille ever imagined. It took Metro-Goldwyn-Mayer to do it.

Outdoor Advertising: How To Do It Right

Outdoor advertising includes posters or billboards, painted walls or buildings, transportation advertising, marquees, window displays and signs on the property itself.

While outdoor advertising is not a "do-it-yourself" project, it doesn't hurt to be knowledgeable about what you should be getting for your money from a professional sign company. For example, the more contrast between the colors of the lettering and the background of your sign, the better. Dark letters against a light background usually result in maximum visibility and readability.

If your sign design is confusing and cluttered, many potential customers won't take the trouble to read the message. To avoid problems, keep letter style simple and avoid script or italic letters except in unusual circumstances. As a rule of thumb, each two inches of letter height adds about a hundred feet to the distance at which a letter can be seen and read. An eight inch letter should be readable, therefore, from as far away as 400 feet. Letters and words must be properly spaced. If they seem to run together at the distance from which most prospects view your sign, you're in trouble.

To get full effectiveness from your sign at night it must be planned to stand out from traffic lights, car headlights and other nearby lighted signs. Experts say that internally illuminated signs are the most efficient and effective for both day and night.

Newspaper and Magazine Advertising

Even more than outdoor advertising, newspaper and magazine advertising call for use of the best professional talent. Again, while leaving the production to the experts, it is useful to be aware of some guiding principles which should be observed.

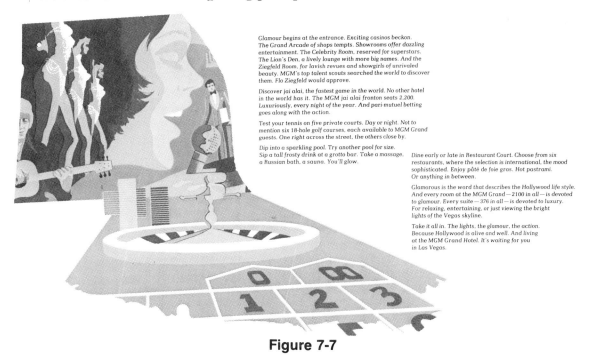

Glamour begins at the entrance. Exciting casinos beckon. The Grand Arcade of shops tempts. Showrooms offer dazzling entertainment. The Celebrity Room, reserved for superstars. The Lion's Den, a lively lounge with more big names. And the Ziegfeld Room, for lavish revues and showgirls of unrivaled beauty. MGM's top talent scouts searched the world to discover them. Flo Ziegfeld would approve.

Discover jai alai, the fastest game in the world. No other hotel in the world has it. The MGM jai alai fronton seats 2,200. Luxuriously, every night of the year. And pari-mutuel betting goes along with the action.

Test your tennis on five private courts. Day or night. Not to mention six 18-hole golf courses, each available to MGM Grand guests. One right across the street, the others close by.

Dip into a sparkling pool. Try another pool for size. Sip a tall frosty drink at a grotto bar. Take a massage, a Russian bath, a sauna. You'll glow.

Dine early or late in Restaurant Court. Choose from six restaurants, where the selection is international, the mood sophisticated. Enjoy pâté de foie gras. Hot pastrami. Or anything in between.

Glamorous is the word that describes the Hollywood life style. And every room at the MGM Grand — 2100 in all — is devoted to glamour. Every suite — 376 in all — is devoted to luxury. For relaxing, entertaining, or just viewing the bright lights of the Vegas skyline.

Take it all in. The lights, the glamour, the action. Because Hollywood is alive and well. And living at the MGM Grand Hotel. It's waiting for you in Las Vegas.

Figure 7-7

The most civilized hotel in New York.
Maybe the world.

The Regency Hotel
Park Avenue at 61st Street, New York, N.Y. 10021. (212) 759-4100

Figure 7-8

Black and white magazine ad prepared by KOEHL, LANDIS, and LANDAN for New York's Regency Hotel was chosen tops in its class in HSMA advertising contest.

A. Media Selection—More important than total number of people reached by a publication is the number of *prospects* who will see an ad since each ad should be aimed at a particular market or prospect group.

B. Repetition—A one-time ad is virtually useless. Advertising gains in effectiveness by repetition.

C. Objective—Each ad should have a specific purpose: attract conventions, develop weekend business, promote food and beverage facilities, etc.. Copy should stick with the point.

D. Appearance—Each ad should not only visually reflect the image of your property, but copy should be appropriately worded for the audience you are trying to reach.

E. Distinctiveness—Whether achieved through use of a symbol or logotype, copy style, illustration or type style—or several of these—an effort should be made to create and stay with an ad personality that will be easily recognizable.

Jack Cleek doesn't fish for compliments.

He knows he does a great job, and he knows you bene-fit from it. That's good enough for him. Jack Cleek is Fishing Supervisor at The Homestead, where the Golf Pro, the Tennis Pro, and everyone from the Manager to the Doorman is equally sensitive to your needs. In the end we believe it's people, not buildings, that make a resort truly great. And the people at The Homestead are like Jack Cleek. Come and meet them soon. You'll discover who makes The Homestead truly great.

HOMESTEAD
HOT SPRINGS, VIRGINIA 24445

America's Favorite Mountain Resort

The Homestead, offers three 18-hole championship golf courses, tennis, swimming, fishing, horse-back riding, ten-pin and lawn bowling, buckboard and surrey driving, a supervised children's playground. The Homestead is easily reached via U.S. Route 220, train service by Amtrak to nearby Clifton Forge or Piedmont Airlines to the Hot Springs Airport. Airport runways accommodate private jet aircraft. See your travel agent or write for free color folder, or call (703) 839-5500.

Figure 7-9

Magazine advertisement above won an award for the Homestead (Agency: Needham & Grohmann, Inc.) in Hotel Sales Management Association contest resort category.

"Yellow Pages" Ads Produce Results

Of the some 33 million people who stayed at or looked for a hotel, motel, cabin, camp or resort in a recent 12-month period, 24 percent made use of the Yellow Pages "Hotels, Motels" listings in telephone directories. According to the survey by an independent research organization which unearthed this statistic, these Yellow Pages users consulted the "Hotels, Motels" listings an average of seven times a person. In view of this intelligence, and the relatively low cost of the medium, innkeepers should not overlook Yellow Pages ads in local telephone directories. Those properties drawing considerable business from the suburbs or a few major cities might consider listings under "Hotels and Motels, Out-of-Town" in the directories serving those areas.

Advertising over the Air

Local radio and TV advertising, while high in cost in major cities, can be quite reasonable and more effective in small communities.

The key to successful use of these media, insofar as hotel/motel advertising is concerned, is frequent use of spot announcements on the days and times of day when your prospects are most likely to be listeners or viewers. Summer resort promotion, for example, would be most effective during late spring months; afternoon and early evening are the best times to reach motorists.

Aside from spot ads to promote room or food and beverage sales, radio and TV offer opportunities to sponsor or participate in a variety of activities with wide-spread listener appeal—local sporting events; programs originating in the hotel such as "Breakfast with ____" and speeches by distinguished individuals; and tie-ins with local promotions of other businesses or organizations.

Advertising Results Should Be Measured

In the final analysis, the only real tests of effective advertising are whether and how much it contributes to sales and its net effect on the profit figure. Measurement of results of image-building advertising is a long-term project, but ads which are designed to trigger an immediate response can and should be evaluated in the days following their appearance. Among the ways a check can be gotten on the pulling power of the latter are couponing ads offering a discount or a complimentary cocktail, requests for additonal information offered in the ad and the increase in sales of a package plan or other promotional offer made by the ad.

Maximizing Your Advertising Dollar

Set aside funds for information gathering and research.
Set attainable market and advertising goals.
Find out what your guests want.
Select the most effective communications media.
Don't cut your advertising budget in lean years.

Carry your message to your specific markets.
Measure the results of your advertising program.
Regularly review your budget, goals, and media mix.

Do Your Sales Letters Really Sell?

Chances are, if you write like most businessmen, your letters are dull, dull, dull. Most writers of business letters—even sales letters—put their creativity and warm personality into the deep freeze the minute they take pen in hand or start dictating. Instead of writing naturally and to the point, most of us get all involved in hackneyed phrases and circumlocution. Here are some practical points for good letters which can't help but improve your sales correspondence:

1. *Plan your letter first.* Don't start writing or talking before thinking. Ask yourself, "Why am I writing this and what do I want to accomplish?"
2. *Capture the reader's attention* with an interesting first sentence.
3. *Write as you would talk.* Would you ever say, "We deem it prudent," in conversation?
4. *Be clear, concise and brief.* How long should a letter be? Exactly long enough to heat the water to a boil.
5. *Use simple action words.* Short sentences and paragraphs impart vitality to a letter.
6. *Be friendly and positive.* When you write a letter you're putting yourself in an envelope to go and talk with the reader. The letter is your substitute for personal contact.
7. *Edit carefully.* You may never know when a poor letter may rise from the grave to haunt you.

Although sales letters should be tailored to the audience and reflect the personality of the writer, as well as play up the unique features of a particular property, a great deal can be gained from a study of sales letters that have worked for others. The Hotel Sales Management Association publication, "Hotel Letters that Sell," a 340 page sample book of proven sales letters and promotional pieces, is an invaluable source of good ideas that can be adapted or improved upon.

One-on-One Selling Is Crucial

Personal selling has been called "the most impelling type of selling." Advertising and promotional materials may soften up the prospect, but the sale, nine times out of ten, comes down to the one person who asks for the order and gets the prospect to sign on the dotted line.

Innumerable books have been written on the secrets of personal selling and virtually all offer sensible advice if not panaceas. Elmer Wheeler's "sell the sizzle, not the steak" has got to rank among the most memorable words ever written about selling. Right alongside them, though, this writer would put the advice: "Don't ask whether or not, ask which one?"

The entire hotel/motel staff should be coached and required to offer sales suggestions to guests whenever opportunities arise. Obvious occasions are:

Room Clerk when guest registers—suggest more expensive room for view, additional comforts; mention food facilities, in-room motion pictures.
Bellman rooming guest—mention specialty restaurants, hotel's entertainment facilities.
Waitress serving meals—suggest specialty of the house, beverages with the meal, featured desserts.

Aside from encouraging the guest to make full use of the facilities of the property, personal selling also has public relations value which can show up in repeat business.

The entire staff at the Century Plaza in Los Angeles, Las Vegas' Frontier, the Atlanta Marriott and the Savoy in London radiate so much sincere friendliness and desire to be helpful to guests that it is worthy of comment.

"Personal selling is the most potent method for promoting hotel sales," according to Henry W. Beardsley, formerly Senior Vice-President-Marketing, Inter-Continental Hotels. "Here the seller has an opportunity to make a complete presentation of his sales story, to answer all objections, and follow through to the completion of a sale with a signed order. This can all occur in one meeting with his prospect."

Guides to Personal Selling Effectiveness

In a manual prepared for its sales managers, Inter-Continental offers the following suggestions:

1. Have a specific reason for making the call. Don't just drop in to exchange pleasantries.
2. Study up on the organization you plan to call on—its products, organization, meeting habits, etc..
3. Plan your selling approach to emphasize benefits to the customer and how your property and service are superior to the competition.
4. Work your sales presentation out carefully and rehearse it so interruptions will not throw you off the track.
5. Strive to get—
    A. A definite commitment
    B. At least a tentative booking.
    C. A commitment from the prospect to inspect your facilities.
6. Leave something with the prospect to aid his recall—a rate card, folder, a small souvenir.
7. *Do* be on time for your appointment.
8. Make sure your prospect knows who you are and the property you represent. Hand him your business card.
9. Be concise. Get to the point. Don't overstay your welcome.

10. Use visual aids such as floor plans, photographs and sample menus to drive your points home.
11. Look at things from the prospect's point of view.
     A. Find out *his* needs
     B. Let *him* set the pace. If he wants details, give him details.
     C. Listen.
12. *Don't* oversell. Leave when you have made the sale or finished your presentation.

Selling by Telephone

Some additional advice, from the same source, for effective telephone selling:

1. Be available, make sure incoming sales calls are routed directly to the sales office. Let associates know where you can be reached.
2. Speak the prospect's language.
3. Ask questions. Find out all you can about the prospect's needs and plans. He may require facilities or service beyond what he is inquiring about.
4. Take notes. Don't trust to memory for correct spelling of a prospect's name, his address and phone number, his requirements and essential follow-up.
5. Don't take "no" for an answer. Try to get an appointment for a personal visit or a commitment to inspect your property.

The Marketing Approach Summarized

In summary, these are the essentials of the marketing approach:

1. *Know your market.* Be tuned in to your potential customers' goals and feelings. This is where research comes in (for example: travel patterns, guest preference studies and guest histories).
2. *Know your competition.* Not only other hotels and motels, but friends and relatives with whom 50% of automobile travelers stay, camping areas, possibly in the future airplanes which will convert to hotels when they land, etc.. Also remember that, for all except business travelers, staying at a hotel or motel is discretionary spending and you are also competing with sellers of jewelry, furs, color TV's, automobiles, etc..
3. *Know your product.* What is distinctive about your property that constitutes a moving and simple selling point? Overselling what you can do for a customer is as bad as overbooking rooms. Be sure you know your property's limitations as well as its capabilities.
4. *Redesign your product* continually to appeal to the changing market and to overcome competition. Keep alert to new opportunities through modernization and redecorating, installation of new products such as in-room motion pictures and automatic food dispensers, creation of package plans to increase weekend business, seeking arrangements for inclusive tour packages with airlines and

travel agents. Be sure your *pricing* is right—low enough to get the business, but high enough to return a fair profit—and that it is competitive with comparable properties. Finally, follow through to guarantee that the customer gets the facilities and service you or your advertising promised.

5. *Use all the marketing tools effectively.* To support your personal selling, make use of or capitalize on the techniques of advertising, direct mail, sales promotion, publicity, etc..

Just as the door-to-door salesman is a relic of a long past era, so the hotel/motel manager or sales manager who does not understand marketing, who does not employ its tools and techniques, is rapidly becoming anachronistic. In the lodging business there is no room for mere order-takers. You have to sell hard and you have to sell effectively. Anyone who tries to make sales without knowing and utilizing the wide range of marketing technology available to him is fighting with one arm tied behind his back.

8

Special Techniques
That Bring in the
Extra Business

A prime source of business for many properties in the years ahead will be visitors from abroad. International tourism tends to develop more rapidly than national tourism and growing affluence overseas, coupled with devaluation of the dollar, are creating an almost exponential increase in the number of people who can afford travel to the U.S.

One measure of the potential of business from overseas is the prediction by the International Union of Official Travel Organizations in Geneva, Switzerland, that "even on a conservative estimate, it is probable that by 1985—provided no other economic, social or political factor disturbs the situation—international tourist demand will have quadrupled since 1965."

Both government and the private sector are making substantial efforts to attract visitors from abroad to the U.S.

In place of the token governmental efforts prior to 1961 to attract international visitors, we now have the U.S. Travel Service which operates on a multi-million dollar budget. While a great improvement over the past, the amount of money allocated by the U.S. for overseas promotion of travel to this country is still considerably less than the promotional budgets for similar purposes of much smaller and less prosperous countries.

Discover America Travel Organizations, Inc., a non-profit agency created by a merger of the National Association of Travel Organizations and Discover America, Inc., promotes travel from abroad as well as domestic tourism.

Perhaps the most active of all have been the airlines—both domestic and international—who have expended many millions of dollars to lure foreign visitors to our shores.

Cashing in on International Tourism

There are many ways hotels and motels interested in developing international business, at little or no cost, can cash in on international tourism opportunities.

- Work with wholesalers to have your property included in package tours.
- Cooperate with airlines and other organizations bringing foreign travel agents and travel writers to this country on familiarization tours.
- Make promotional material available for distribution overseas in the language of the country where it is to be disseminated.
- Special interest groups overseas are an important source of business. With more than 100 "Wild West" clubs in Europe, there is a ready-made market for tours of our western states. Fall foliage tours and historical site tours are other possibilities.
- Provide special promotional rates for international visitors, particularly if they can be encouraged to come during slack periods.
- "Extend the invitation" by advertising in directories travel agents overseas use in planning hotel accommodations for their clients.
- Write directly to those overseas travel agents sending significant numbers of their clients to the U.S. A list for this purpose is obtainable from the United States Travel Service.
- Utilize services of hotel representatives abroad.
- Since many Americans belong to international groups which have never had a convention in the U.S., ask your business clients to urge the international groups to which they belong to hold their next convention in this country. Better yet, make a direct approach to the heads of foreign associations and other convention holders.

Serving the International Visitor

As for serving the international visitor, a publication of the American Hotel & Motel Association offers these suggestions:

1. Correspondence from abroad should be answered promptly and in the language of the person who has written.
2. Do something about the language problem. a. Utilize the language skills of your employees as interpreters. b. Provide employees and foreign guests with phrase books which give English translations of a travel vocabulary for most commonly encountered languages. c. Have menus available in at least French, German, Italian and Spanish. d. Provide for easy and fair currency exchange. e. Have available tape recorders with foreign language tapes to be used on local walking tours. f. In handling group tours, pre-register members of the party, be sure all members of the group understand meal and tipping arrangements, and that all accounts are settled before departure.

"A Picture Is Worth More . . ."

One of the big "hang-ups" of many potential travelers to the U.S. is a fear of the language barrier here. To aid travelers who do not understand English, the International Committee for Breaking the Language Barrier advocates the use of symbols on signs.

The essentials of good signing to overcome the language barrier are these, according to ICBLB:

1. *Give information.* An example is the implementation in New York City of an ICBLB recommendation that route diagrams be put up at bus stops. As a result, non-English speaking visitors can determine which bus to board and what route it will take.
2. *Use basic vocabulary.* The word "lounge," for instance, can confuse international visitors because it is used here for bar, lobby and also toilet.
3. *Make multi-lingual signs.* But keep in mind that, since all major languages can't be included because of space, graphic symbols should also be included. Airports at San Francisco and Seattle, for example, combine both symbols and language to indicate facilities.
4. *Make objects visible.* The language problem can be eased by showing the item itself rather than trying to describe it. For example, salt and pepper could be packaged in transparent envelopes. Some restaurants abroad display wax models of food they serve.
5. *Illustrate.* Rather than wait until international standardized symbols are universally agreed upon, use some form of graphics to convey messages. While graphic communication may not be perfect, it will be better than words which do not communicate at all.
6. *Use Maps.* They speak a universal language. Many places in Europe post large city maps in railway stations. In Tokyo, neighborhood maps are posted at major street intersections and at police stations.
7. *Use international symbols* wherever practical. Visitors from overseas complain about traffic signs here because they vary among different states and cities. Today, many internationally-minded cities such as Tokyo, Montreal and Frankfurt use international symbols instead of the local language.

Figure 8-1

Symbols pictured are among those recommended by the International Air Transport Association for use at airports and in other locations where international travelers might be in need of information. Symbols are in black on white background except for shaded portions of signs which are in red.

A "Can't Lose" Proposition

One of the best ways for a hotel or motel to capture a share of the international travel market is through participation in a "sell and report" or "free sale" arrangement with international airlines. As the name implies, this arrangement permits the overseas offices of the airlines with whom agreement is reached to immediately confirm to clients bookings for rooms in the property at agreed upon rates and subject to certain advance notice limitations. The airline advises the hotel or motel of the booking promptly. If space should not be available, the airline notifies the client and offers alternative accommodations. This service is provided by the airlines at no charge to the hotel or motel for commission, communication or listing. If a travel agent overseas makes the reservation through the airline, and the property normally pays commissions, it would, of course, be expected to pay a commission to the agent.

Soliciting Group Business

Group business accounts for as much as 35 percent of the sales volume in major hotels and around 15 percent in smaller properties. Many resort hotels would have to close their doors permanently were it not for group business, especially meetings and conventions scheduled for the pre and post-"season" periods.

There are five basic types of group business:

A. Conventions
B. Sales meetings, seminars, etc.
C. Incentive travel groups
D. Tourists
E. Special interest

Conventions are, of course, big business. On an average, there are more than 35,000 national, regional and intra-state conventions held annually in the U.S.. Conventions generate an estimated two billion dollars in gross sales directly and probably at least as much indirectly.

Compared to the vacation visitor, who spends 24 percent of his dollar (apart from transportation) on hotel rooms and about four percent in hotel restaurants, according to the New York Convention and Visitors Bureau, the convention delegate spends 30 percent of his dollar for hotel rooms and 10 percent in hotel restaurants, plus five percent additional for beverages.

Two other facts underline the importance of convention business to hotel profitability: (1) the overall cost in time and money of attracting 100 to 2,000 individual guests is much greater than the cost of signing up one convention with the same number of delegates, and (2) individual travelers are far more likely to cancel reservations or be "no-shows" than convention delegates.

Sales meetings and other corporate meetings held in public facilities in the U.S. top 300,000 a year. Annual expenditures for such meetings—plus trade shows and exhibitions—are well over $4 billion. Attendance ranges from less than 10 for training meetings and management development seminars to nearly 200 for national sales meetings. Most meetings are of several days duration.

Sites for corporate meetings may be selected from any of the following: (1) headquarters city, (2) geographic center of sales or executive force, (3) center of product market area, (4) in a potential market area, (5) in a resort area or (6) where hotels or meeting centers provide the latest in meeting facilities. Because of their dispersion geographically, and the generally small number of participants, corporate meetings should be looked upon as a prime source of revenue by every hotel or motel, no matter how small.

Incentive travel is becoming an increasingly important factor in the travel industry. Participants in incentive travel groups may be as few as 15 and as many as 6,000. The average incentive trip lasts five days. Total annual expenditures for incentive travel are nearly $½ billion. While holidays abroad are the most popular form of incentive travel, there is no reason why American hotels and motels can't recapture a share of this business in view of currency exchange problems, inflation, and political unrest in many countries overseas.

Group tourist travel is a world-wide phenomenon. It has been increasing at a rate of nearly 20 percent a year.

Since the packagers of group tours—the wholesale travel agency or the tour operator—are the ones who "put it all together," properties desiring to bid for this business should make this desire known to them, along with information about facilities, services, and rates which would lure international or domestic visitors as the case might be.

In addition to the categories mentioned so far, there is one more—*special interest groups*—which are, or could be, likely prospects. Examples are: university seminars or workshops; technical meetings; Board of Directors meetings; sports or hobby groups such as skiers, skin divers, and golfers; amateur archeologists; Civil War buffs, etc.

Groups may be organized by a member, a travel agent may either arrange or initiate the trip, an airline might provide the impetus, or the hotel/motel itself could be the moving force.

Criteria Checklist for Group Selection

A major international hotel chain establishes these criteria to help maximize profitability from group business:

1. Evaluate carefully reservations for each group requesting space during periods of high occupancy.
2. Give preference to a high-budget business organization staying for five or six days and requiring several formal luncheon meetings or banquets over a limited-budget tourist group, the members of which will take most of their meals in the coffee shop or outside the hotel.
3. Double occupancy is preferred to single occupancy; long stays to short; superior rooms to minimum, etc.
4. On occasion, the choice of groups may depend on a balancing of two factors: revenue produced versus group image. You may wish to accept a group with a good name and reputation (and one whose members will behave well as guests) over a group of dubious reputation, but with a large revenue potential.

Four Group Sales Essentials

Two excellent monographs, *Convention Liaison Manual* and the Hotel Sales Management Association's *Convention Solicitation*, provide detailed information on attracting and handling group business. From the latter come these four essentials in developing an effective sales program designed to attract group business.

1. *Top-level participation.* Management should acquire a good knowledge of this type of business, its value and inherent problems.
2. *Policy consultation.* Your sales staff should have a voice in policy formulation, advertising and other activities where their experience and ideas can be of value.
3. *Full access to information.* Sales staff should be told about operational problems which might affect standards of service committed to group business buyers. Especially important is that they be aware of the physical limitations of the facility, but also the point beyond which standards of service cannot be raised without reducing or eliminating profits.
4. *Keeping sales commitments.* Everyone in the hotel or motel has a responsibility to see that promises made to group business buyers are kept.

How to Keep Groups Happy

Critics of the way hotels and motels handle group business seem to be legion. Among the comments they have offered at conclaves of innkeepers and in the trade press are these:

- Pre-register participants whenever possible; in any case have procedures and adequate numbers of registration personnel to avoid long lines of people waiting for room assignments.
- Be sure there is available to the group *at all times* a member of the staff *with full authority*.
- Don't depart from established rates.
- Plan guest traffic to avoid confusion and congestion at the conclusion of large meetings.
- Have adequate—*and functioning*—equipment for audio-visual presentations (screens, room darkening equipment, public address system, lighted lecterns, etc.).
- Provide detailed floor plans of meeting and exhibit areas.
- "Based on the design and physical facilities of *new American hotels*, we can conclude that American hotel management does not recognize that the most rapidly growing source of group business are informational and educational-type meetings."
- In general, the American hotel industry is not geared or organized to provide the services required to successfully conduct group meetings.
- Hotel salesmen must learn to sell the total community in which their hotel is located, *not* just their physical facilities.
- Provide meeting planners with *specifics* on facilities—exact room sizes and realistic seating capacities.
- Give group business buyers information about meeting rooms, guest rooms, elevator service first. They are more interested in these data than facts on cocktail lounges, lobbies, etc.

- Don't ignore the fact that the group business market is *not a single market*—but a composite of many . . .each with different characteristics and requirements. (There's also an important difference between association conventions and company meetings in *profitability* as well as in selling and servicing. Such things as assured occupancy with company meetings and single billing add to their profitability).

Even though most hotelmen think of group business in terms of large properties and large numbers of participants, size need not be a deterrent to booking appropriate groups. "Many smaller motor hotels and resorts with limited facilities have been able to do a substantial amount of group business by selective marketing," according to Phil Harrison, publisher of *Sales Meetings*. "They have analyzed the needs of the companies and associations whose needs and patterns match their facilities. With intelligent staff training and a coordinated sales program, group business has been booked."

"Filling the House" on Weekends

Given the fact that most hotels and motels, except in resort areas, draw the bulk of their patronage from business travelers, it is not surprising that, while up through the middle of the week, occupancy is at an acceptable or even high level, it turns down drastically on Friday, Saturday and Sunday.

The problem of how to sell rooms on weekends is a persistent, but far from insoluble, one. Innovative hoteliers who have put their minds to it have been able to boost weekend occupancy by as much as 35 percent. Approaches have varied, but in virtually all cases the key element has been the adage, "find a need and fill it."

One of the most rewarding sales ploys to increase weekend business is the "package" —room, meals, some extra touches for glamour, and all at a special price.

The Marriott Hotel chain has had good results with its weekend promotions. Vice President of Sales and Marketing W. W. "Bud" Grice says, "Getting two-thirds or half of the price for a room and meals is better than having rooms and restaurants empty and still having to pay salaries, utilities and taxes."

Other pluses from weekend business are the word-of-mouth advertising by pleased guests and extra revenue from food, liquor and extra-cost activities not included in the package price.

One logical source of weekend profits is businessmen who have been guests previously. A letter addressed to them suggesting they treat their wives to an "escape" weekend can pay big dividends. Or radio and suburban newspaper messages directed to wives holding out the promise of "escape from the drudgery of cleaning and cooking" may be the way to get the ball rolling.

Other possible sources of weekend business are people looking for new homes or apartments, club groups coming into town for a matinee, affluent shoppers and—if the property has a pool, sauna, tennis courts or golf privileges—the sports minded.

The promotion-oriented Dunfey Family has had considerable success with its

"Mini-Vacation" concept offering "the greatest getaway you've ever gone on, a chance to get away with a lot you haven't been able to get away with in a long time."

In addition to three nights at any one Dunfey Hotel, or a different one every night, the plan allows children in the same room without charge and includes full course breakfasts for two.

One of the first weekend packages–and one of the most complete–was that put together by the Conrad Hilton Hotel in Chicago. It included a bottle of champagne, motion picture tickets, a city tour, certain meals, a complimentary cocktail and dancing in the hotel's supper club. A similar package is offered by the Hilton's Waldorf Astoria with its "Weekend at the Waldorf."

Motels on the fringes of cities that are affected by TV blackouts of professional football games have hit "pay dirt" by renting rooms on Sunday afternoons to groups of sports fans who usually turn out to be lavish spenders on food and beverages.

The Northfield Inn in Massachusetts even manages to get many of its fall chores done for free by guests lured there by promises of a work and fun weekend.

How to Raise Occupancy from 12% to a Full House

Probably the most successful weekend promotions in the country are those staged by the Chalfonte-Haddon Hall in Atlantic City, New Jersey. According to Executive Vice President and General Manager Anthony M. Rey, their "special" weekend promotions have built occupancy on certain winter weekends from less than 200 guests to a full house of some 1,700.

Built around a "foreign weekend" theme, the promotions use elaborate sets to create the appropriate "Parisian," "South Seas" or "Caribbean" atmosphere. The staff wears costumes in keeping with the theme area and the food and entertainment as well are appropriately "foreign." Because of the elaborateness of all facets of the program, Rey says, the package plan rates, which have built into them the cost of entertainment and decor, are actually higher than the resort's regular prices.

Direct mail letters and brochures are employed in promoting the special weekends, as are newspaper, radio and TV advertising concentrated in the areas from which most guests are drawn (60 percent come from Philadelphia).

Aside from the direct revenue attributable to the special weekend packages, Rey lists these benefits:

1. In a seasonal resort, it allows management to keep employees on a year 'round basis.
2. Hotel shops get extra business and this, in turn, increases rental income from them.
3. The special weekends serve as a showcase for convention managers and other sources of group business.
4. Guests for special weekends often become regular patrons and provide word of mouth advertising among their friends and associates.

Multiplying Your Sales Force

One motel chain puts on local sales campaigns by having not only the innkeeper, but waitresses, bartenders and other employees call on local prospects to break the ice. The most likely to become sources of business are visited a day or two later by the motel's professional salesman.

Apart from employees, travel agents, tour operators, airlines and hotel representatives all can make positive contributions to keeping occupancy high. In all cases, it is vital that published rates are adhered to rigidly. Where commissions are involved, they should be paid promptly.

Many properties have a problem with under or over-supply of promotional brochures to the offices of travel agents. For a charge that, in most cases, is lower than distribution costs if a property were to do the job itself, a company headquartered on the West Coast will undertake to keep a screened list of travel agents, specially selected for a particular property, provided with an optimum supply of the hotel's promotional brochures.

Travel agents are a significant factor in booking of resort business. Some resort properties report that 30 percent or more of their bookings come to them from travel agents. As pleasure travelers overtake business travelers as the main source of income for non-resort hotels and motels, it may be expected that travel agents will play a more dominant role in providing bookings for these properties as well.

Travel agents are critical of the lodging industry, a survey conducted by *Travel Weekly* disclosed, for brochures failing to give explicit price and tour-feature information; no expiration date on seasonal offerings; and poorly timed distribution. A "must," the majority of agents said, was space—preferably on the front cover—for agency imprint.

According to the survey, half of all unsolicited literature is discarded, 80 percent of display units furnished by suppliers are thrown away.

Airlines can boost occupancy in two ways. The first is referrals by airline personnel asked by travelers to suggest a good place to stay at their destination. The other is the inclusion of a particular property in one of the many tour packages the airlines are constantly developing and aggressively merchandising.

Working either on a fee or commission arrangement, hotel representatives can be extremely helpful in bringing in lucrative group business; promoting the represented property through brochures, advertising and promotional cocktail parties, lunches, etc.; and providing an out-of-town reservation service.

One other valuable source of group business, and for some properties it may be the best, is the tour operator. As Arthur Tauck, a leading tour operator, points out: "Most conventions and meetings must be sold individually and this costs money. For tours, you sell the tour operator only once and, if you attend properly to this business, you receive it year after year like an annuity."

Don't Overlook Your Own Back Yard

Some of the best prospects for increased occupancy may be right in your own community. Here's a suggested contact list:

sales managers of local businesses	bus line personnel
secretaries to local executives	cab drivers
purchasing agents	vendors
civic club officers	funeral parlor directors
clergymen	caterers
officers of women's clubs	near-by colleges and research facilities
service station operators	attractions
rental car agents	

Working to Improve the Community

In addition to being a source of business itself, the local community provides the ambience in which the hotel or motel operates. In his own self interest, the enterprising innkeeper should cooperate with other local businesses and groups in capitalizing on the nation-wide tourism boom. Among the steps to be taken are these:

1. *Improve the product.* Attention needs to be paid to engendering a spirit of hospitality among all community residents and businessmen, not just hotel/motel employees. Properties must be kept attractive and clean and pollution of all kinds reduced. Fair dealing must become the watchwords of all in the community impacting on the tourist business.
2. *Develop attractions.* People on the go need a *reason* to stop overnight in a particular community. Scenic and historic sites and cultural events provide reasons. Those that exist should be made more attractive and convenient to see. Special activities at raceways, harness tracks, amusement parks, wax museums and other gathering points, etc. will stop the traffic. You don't need a Disney World to capture the tourist's attention.
3. *Promote.* Utilize all appropriate media to advertise, publicize, promote —locally, sectionally, nationally.

"Going It Alone" Gets Tougher All the Time

More and more, travelers plan their whole trip far in advance of departure. Not only that, they are becoming increasingly discriminating as to quality of accommodations and meals, availability of a pool or other recreational activity and assured reservations at a set price.

For these reasons, the tourist who drives until sunset and then stops at the first motel displaying a vacancy sign is rapidly becoming a *rara avis*.

Today, the great majority of hotels and motels either are chain owned or managed, franchised, or members of a referral group. In the highly competitive accommodations market, even an unusually well endowed property needs all the marketing help it can get.

Referral groups such as Friendship Inns promote member properties by advertising in national publications and other media and by issuing directories of members which are given large-scale distribution by oil companies and others in contact with the touring public. Many of them make outdoor identification signs available to members. Some also operate a reservation service free to guests of member properties. Referral groups demand that members come up to minimum standards established by the groups in respect to room layout and facilities, availability of food service, etc..

Franchise organizations, in addition to providing all the promotion and services of referral groups and more also offer construction advice, financing assistance, central purchasing and accounting, training courses, etc.. They also go a step further than referral organizations with respect to predictable decor, swimming pool, restaurant, etc. as well as standards of service. Holiday Inns and Howard Johnson's are two of the most ubiquitous franchise groups.

Stephen W. Brener, Senior Vice President-Hospitality Consultant Division, Helmsley-Spear, Inc., offers these suggestions for choosing a referral or franchise group affiliation:

1. Choose one that caters to the type of guest compatible with your operation.
2. Check members to find out their opinion of the groups you are considering.
3. Avoid a franchise or referral group which already has a member close by unless you think you might both benefit by sharing overflow business.
4. Look for one with a successful member or members in your market area which can provide you with referrals.
5. Evaluate costs of conversion or upgrading to meet group requirements as against probable benefits.
6. Make sure the organization is financially sound, that member earnings have been as purported and that it has a record of keeping its promises.
7. Check out the reservation system the group offers. Is it reliable, economical?
8. Ascertain whether mandatory services will cost you a great deal more than they are worth to you.
9. Find out the group's policy on protection against bad accounts.

"New Money" Use Grows

"Travel now-pay later" is an accepted part of the American way of life. Credit cards issued for travel and entertainment, by banks and by major oil companies are used by more than half of all business and pleasure travelers. They are used most frequently to pay for accommodations. Because of their popularity, credit cards have to be considered a sales tool. Not only does their acceptance bring in business a property might not otherwise receive, but an ancillary benefit comes from the promotion by the card issuing companies of properties honoring their cards.

Reservation Systems Continue Struggle

Looked upon a few years ago as a "cure-all" for the ills of the lodging industry, electronic reservation systems have had hard going. Well over a dozen have fallen by the wayside, with losses running to many millions of dollars.

Accommodations Directories and Rating

Apart from the membership directories issued by the various chains, referral groups and franchise organizations, there are several other hotel/motel listings of value. One is the *Red Book*, a publication of the American Hotel & Motel Association, which confines its listings to the more than 8,000 AH&MA member properties. The AAA regional directories and the *Mobil Guides* also are respected listings although they are limited to selected properties. Because it is published quarterly rather than annually, *Hotel & Travel Index*, a worldwide hotel guide, is more current than these other directories. It contains over 21,000 accommodations listings, information on commissions paid to travel agents, and other data of interest to travelers and members of the travel industry. A loose leaf publication in two volumes is the *Official Hotel and Resort Guide* which gives more data than most other directories. Updating is frequent through the mailing to subscribers of substitute or new pages as changes warrant.

Even though many European countries rate their hotels officially or through publications such as the *Guides Michelin*, rating has never been considered practical by American hoteliers. The chief reason they give for their point of view is that rating standards tend to be either extremely rigid or else largely subjective. How, they ask, can one adequately compare the ambience and service of the historic Hay-Adams in Washington with the undeniable plethora of conveniences provided, albeit in a sterile atmosphere, by some more modern properties?

9

Making It as a
Successful Innkeeper

In the final analysis, despite the emphasis on hospitality and service—and rightly so—running a hotel or motel is a *business*. Unless the results in the southeast corner of the profit and loss statement are favorable, no amount of praise or appreciation will insure the survival of the enterprise.

In a word, the touchstone of success as an innkeeper is "profitability."

Obviously profitability doesn't just happen. It must be planned for, carefully nurtured and meticulously controlled. The name of the game is "money management."

Two documents make up the score card of the business. The Balance Sheet (or Statement of Financial Condition) is usually prepared at year end and is a summary of the enterprise's assets, liabilities and owner's equity as of a particular date.

EXHIBIT A

BALANCE SHEET

AT_____ , 19____

ASSETS

CURRENT ASSETS
    Cash on Hand ....$
    Cash in Banks ....
    Notes Receivable ....
    Accounts Receivable...$
      Less Provision for Un-
      collectible Accounts .... _____
    Inventories of Saleable Merchandise...
    Deposits on Purchase Commitments...
    Marketable Securities (Temporary
      Investments)...
    Prepaid Expenses ....
    Other Current Assets.. _____
      Total Current Assets...$

FUNDS, DEPOSITS AND INVESTMENTS
  Deposits with Public Utilities
    Corporations...$
  Funds Deposited with Trustees.....................................
  Cash Surrender Value of Life Insurance........................
  Stocks, Bonds and Other Securities .... _____
      Total Funds, Deposits and Investments..............................$

CAPITAL ASSETS
  Land...$
  Land Improvements..$
    Less: Accumulated
      Depreciation .... _____
  Buildings and
    Improvements..
    Less: Accumulated
      Depreciation...................................... _____
  Furniture, Furnishings
    and Equipment..
    Less: Accumulated
      Depreciation...................................... _____
  Leasehold and
    Improvements..
    Less: Accumulated
      Amortization...................................... _____
  Linens and Uniforms .... _____
      Total Capital Assets..$

OTHER ASSETS
  Organization and Financing Costs...$
  Goodwill..
  Other... _____
      Total Other Assets .... _____
TOTAL ASSETS...$ ========

Liabilities and Capital

CURRENT LIABILITIES
  Notes and Accounts Payable...$
  Installment Contracts Payable
    (Due within one year) ....
  Taxes Collected..
  Employee Taxes...
  Taxes Payable...
  Dividends Payable..
  Accrued Liabilities...
  Deposits from Guests on Room and
    Exchange Reservations..
  Mortgages Payable: Due
    within one year..
  Other Current Liabilities.. _____
      Total Current Liabilities..$

LONG TERM INDEBTEDNESS
  Mortgages..$
  Other Long Term Notes and Debts.......................... _____
      Total Long Term Debts..$

CAPITAL (If A Corporation)
  Capital Stock Outstanding
    Preferred ....$
    Common ....

Retained Earnings (Or Deficit) .... _____
     Total Capital .... $ _____

OWNER'S EQUITY (If a
Partnership or individual .... $ _____   _____
     Total Owner's Equity .... _____

TOTAL LIABILITIES AND CAPITAL .... $ _____

The Profit and Loss Statement, (or Operating Statement) which is usually made up monthly, is a summary of income and expense transactions taking place during the period covered.

EXHIBIT B

OPERATING STATEMENT

(name of business)

to

(period covered)

	Current Period	Per-cent	Accu-mulated	Per-cent
REVENUE				
Room sales .... $ _____		100.%	$ _____	100.%
CONTROLLABLE OPERAT-ING EXPENSES				
Salaries and wages				
Manager (or owner-manager allowance) .... $		%	$	%
Employees				
Payroll taxes and employee benefits	_____		_____	
Subtotal .... $		%	$	%
Laundry, dry cleaning and Uniforms				
Linen Costs				
Guest room supplies				
Cleaning Supplies				
Advertising and business promotion				
Commissions, discounts and allowances				
Dues, subscriptions and contributions				
Telephone, telegraph				
Office supplies, services and postage				
Traveling and automobile expenses				
Fuel, water and electricity				
Repairs and maintenance				
Cash over/short				
Other operating expenses	_____	_____	_____	_____
Total controllable operating expenses .... $	_____	%	$ _____	%

	Current Period	Percent	Accumulated	Percent
GROSS OPERATING INCOME FROM ROOMS	$ _____	__ %	$ _____	__ %
OTHER SOURCES OF INCOME				
Gross profit from merchandise sales	$	%	$	%
Income from food services (net)				
Income from vending machines (less costs)				
Income from leased facilities				
Other income	_____		_____	
Total other income	$ _____	__ %	$ _____	__ %
PROFIT AVAILABLE FOR FIXED EXPENSES, INSURANCE & TAXES	$ _____	__ %	$ _____	__ %
FIXED EXPENSES				
Rent—land and buildings	$	%	$	%
Rent—equipment and furnishings				
Licenses and taxes				
Insurance				
Interest				
Depreciation and amortization				
Total fixed expenses	$ _____	__ %	$ _____	__ %
NET INCOME (OR LOSS) FROM OPERATIONS	$ _____	__ %	$ _____	__ %
OTHER ADDITIONS AND DEDUCTIONS	$ _____	__ %	$ _____	__ %
NET INCOME (OR LOSS) before income taxes and ownership distribution	$ _____	__ %	$ _____	__ %

Together these reports are the finger on the financial pulse of the organization. They are the keys to budgeting, sales and expense analysis, controls and forecasts. It is the job of the accountant to prepare these reports and to assist management in interpreting what the figures mean in terms of future decision-making.

A useful tool in financial analysis is this pro forma Revenue and Expense Statement. In using it, dollar amounts go in the first column and the second column shows the percentage of each item relative to room sales.

EXHIBIT C

REVENUE:		
Room Sales	$ _____	100%
CONTROLLABLE OPERATING EXPENSES:		
Manager's Salary (or Owner's Allowance)	_____	_____
Employee's Wages and Salaries	_____	_____
Payroll Taxes, Ins. and Benefits	_____	_____
Total Wages and Benefits	_____	_____
Laundry and Dry Cleaning	_____	_____

Linen Cost (Consumed, Replacements, Rentals).. _____ _____
Guest Room Supplies... _____ _____
Cleaning Supplies.. _____ _____
Advertising and Sales Promotion .... _____ _____
Commissions, Discounts, and Allowances... _____ _____
Telephone and Telegraph .... _____ _____
Dues, Subscriptions, and Contributions... _____ _____
Fuel, Electricty, and Water .... _____ _____
Travel and Automotive Expenses.. _____ _____
Repairs and Maintenance.. _____ _____
Office Supplies, Services, and Postage.. _____ _____
Cash Over and Short.. _____ _____
Other Operating Expenses... _____ _____
    Total Controllable Operating Expenses..$ _____ _____
GROSS OPERATING REVENUE FROM ROOMS ....$ _____ _____
MISCELLANEOUS SOURCES OF INCOME ....$ _____ _____
Gross Profit from Merchandise Sales .... _____ _____
Income from Food Service .... _____ _____
Income from Vending Machines.. _____ _____
Income from Leased Facilities... _____ _____
Other Income.. _____ _____
    Total Miscellaneous Income...$ _____ _____

PROFIT AVAILABLE FOR FIXED EXPENSES AND TAXES..........................$ _____ _____

FIXED EXPENSES:
Rent—Land and Buildings.. _____ _____
Rent—Equipment and Furnishings.. _____ _____
Insurance .... _____ _____
Taxes—Other than Income Tax .... _____ _____
Licenses .... _____ _____
Interest Expense... _____ _____
Depreciation .... _____ _____
Amortization—Intangibles .... _____ _____
    Total Fixed Expenses..$ _____ _____
NET INCOME FROM OPERATIONS ....$ _____ _____

How to Bolster Cash Flow

In order to maintain liquidity and to optimize profitability, the hotel manager must assure himself of an adequate cash flow—profit after taxes. This can be accomplished in a variety of ways.

1. *Expense Reduction*—Cutting waste and spoilage, better utilization of manpower, astute purchasing.
2. *Sales Improvement*—Tapping new markets, getting guests to stay longer and come more frequently, promoting high profit beverage sales.
3. *Freeing Up Cash*—Holding inventories low, keeping a close watch on receivables, leasing rather than purchasing.
4. *Financial Management*—borrowing funds at a rate lower than the return you can make them earn, utilizing the principle of leverage.
5. *Increasing Prices*—Rates should reflect increases in costs but need to be competitive. Because of fixed overhead, a small increase in prices could mean a substantial rise in profits.

Break-Even Analysis

Whether decisions need to be made on pricing, costs or capital improvements, the break-even concept is an important aid. Break-even has been defined as "that point in the business year when total cumulative Revenue equals fixed expenses for the year plus the variable expenses up to that date."

To illustrate the application of this concept, assume a motel with fixed expenses of $75,000 annually and variable costs representing 40% of the room rate.

$$\frac{\text{Fixed Expenses}}{(100\% - \% \text{ Variable Costs})} = \frac{\text{Break-even}}{\text{Sales}} \quad \frac{\$75,000}{(100\%-40\%)} = \frac{\$75,000}{60\%} = \$125,000$$

The Break-Even Room Sales Point for this property would be $125,000. If the motel had 100 rooms and an average room rate of $12.50, the motel would have to rent 10,000 rooms during the year to break even. Available rooms for the year (100x365) are 36,500. Break-even occupancy rate would be less than 28% (10,000 divided by 36,500).

This formula can be used to determine the break-even occupancy at various rates. Obviously, since costs are not significantly affected by higher occupancy, the higher the average room rate charged, the lower the percentage of occupancy needed to break even.

Break-Even Analysis can also be used to determine the effect on the break-even sales point of improving facilities (reflected as a change in Fixed Expenses in the formula), and to gauge the effect of increases in Variable Costs such as pay increases for maids or extras provided in guest rooms.

Example: A motor inn owner was considering whether to enlarge and redecorate his cocktail lounge. He wanted to know what monthly sales would have to be for the upgraded facility to break even. What would volume have to reach in order for him to realize a $1,000 a month profit on the operation?

Allocated cost of space, redecorating and additional equipment (amortized over a five year period) he estimated would total $8,000 a year. Additional salaries and overhead he figured at $10,000 a year:

    Annual fixed costs $18,000
    Monthly fixed costs (1/12) $1,500

Assuming variable cost per drink to be 50¢ or 40 percent of drinks priced at $1.25, the break-even point would be 2,000 drinks a month.

(monthly fixed costs) $\dfrac{\$1,500}{.75}$ = 2,000 drinks break-even point
(profit per drink)

To earn a $1,000 a month profit on the operation:

$\dfrac{\$1,000}{.75}$ (expected profit) = 1,333 drinks a month *above* the break-even point
(unit profit)

2,000 drinks a month to break even
<u>1,333</u> additional drinks per month
3,333 drinks a month to realize $1,000 profit

The break-even concept is illustrated graphically on next page:

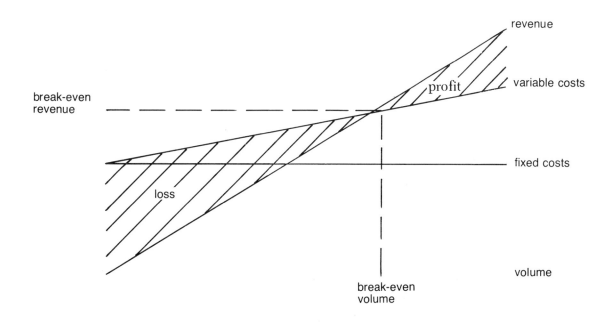

Break-even analysis is a particularly useful tool in preparing feasibility studies. An actual example of such an analysis prepared for a client by a major hotel/motel accounting firm is reproduced below:

STATEMENT OF PROJECTED ANNUAL INCOME AND EXPENSES AT BREAK-EVEN POINT BEFORE MANAGEMENT FEE

	At annual occupancy level of 45.6%	
	Amount	Ratio
Total sales:		
Rooms	$3,585,500	50.0%
Food	1,810,700	25.3
Beverages	452,700	6.3
Telephone	43,000	.6
Golf	503,500	7.0
Other operated departments	739,600	10.3
Other income	35,900	.5
	7,170,900	100.0
Cost of goods sold and departmental wages and expenses:		
Rooms	1,153,200	32.2
Food and beverages	1,508,000	66.6
Telephone	59,000	137.2
Golf	265,100	52.7
Other operated departments	492,600	66.6
	3,477,900	48.5
Gross operating income	3,693,000	51.5

Deductions from income:
Administrative and general (excluding
  management fee) 490,100 13.6
Advertising and sales promotion 325,000 9.1
Heat, light and power 314,800 8.8
Repairs and maintenance 441,800 12.3
  1,571,700 43.8*

House profit (GOP) before real estate taxes,
  fire insurance, rent and management fee 2,121,300 29.6

Real estate taxes 8,400 .1
Insurance 70,400 1.0
Rent 2,042,500 28.5
  2,121,300 29.6
Profit before management fee $ — — %

Average daily rate per occupied room $ 61.50

*Ratio to room sales

Good financial management in the lodging industry is primarily a matter of sound planning and strict control. Areas where appropriate control can make a significant contribution to profitability are food service, beverage service and payroll and other operating expense.

Eleven Ways to Control Food Service Costs

To control food service costs consideration should be given to these time-tested suggestions:

1. Reduce number of items offered on the menu.
2. Feature cooked-to-order items.
3. Concentrate on serving one main category of guest such as businessmen or young people.
4. Limit hours of service.
5. Control portions carefully.
6. Base sales forecast on past experience.
7. Purchase competitively.
8. Take advantage of seasonal food bargains.
9. Check quantity, quality and billing of food items delivered.
10. Avoid spoilage as a result of improper storage.
11. Prevent unauthorized use of food supplies.

How to Use the "Range Report"

A popular and effective food cost accounting system which is particularly useful for the small to medium size operation is the "Range Report." It consists of four simple steps.
1. Determine how many portions of each of the main entree items go to the cooks each day.

2. Count how many portions of each entree item are paid for at the cashiers.
3. Count the number of left over portions in the kitchen at the end of the day.
4. A comparison of these three amounts should show that what went into the kitchen was either paid for by guests or is available for use the next day.

RANGE REPORT						Date:
Menu Item and Portion Specification	Sales Order Fore- cast	Kitchen Product Order Invent.	Left- Overs	Total Sales per Kitch.	Total Sales per Cash.	Short or (Over)
Veal Chop—1 Each	20	18	2	16	16	—
Salmon Steak—6 oz. Raw	30	35	10	25	24	1
Roast Turkey—5 oz. Cooked	25	25	Out 8 p.m.	25	28	(3)
Roast Rib—8 oz. Cooked	50	44	12	32	25	7
Filet Steak—6 oz. Raw	20	24	2	22	31	1
Totals	145	146	26	120	114	6
Fried Chicken—Substitute for Turkey	—	—	—	12	12	—
Totals	145	146	26	132	126	6

Controlling Beverage Service Costs

While similar in many ways, insofar as management is concerned, to food service, beverage service presents somewhat different control problems. One major difference, of course, is the requirement of complying with federal, state and local regulations regarding hours of sale, age of customers and reports to be submitted.

As with food service, beverage cost control begins with an analysis of the potential customer who will offer the best chance for profit for the particular property and then specializes in securing that type of customer.

Since quantity discounts on liquor purchases can be sizable, it is advantageous to limit the number of brands offered, guided by the tastes of regular customers.

Portion control, especially important with a high profit item such as liquor, is facilitated by use of dispensers or bottled individual servings of liquor and beer rather than service by the glass.

Even though there is little or no spoilage problem with beverages, it is necessary to have accurate monthly forecasts to avoid tying up money in liquor inventory and, at the same time, to insure adequate supplies of brands to avoid running out at a critical time. A good rule of thumb is that total liquor inventory should not exceed the value of one month's cost of goods sold.

There are a number of beverage control systems in current use. One, the *Cost of Goods Sold Percentage System*, has a couple of major drawbacks. Since it depends on the taking of inventory, the results are not known until several weeks after the close of the period. And, since the overall figure is the total of many individual transactions at different mark-ups, it can be skewed by unusual sales mixes.

Another beverage control method which is effective is the *Daily Inventory Control System*. This requires taking a bar inventory at the end of each day. It not only is an aid to improved profitability, but helps in becoming more aware of the operating problems of the beverage function. The obvious disadvantage of this system is the time it takes to inventory and calculate usage.

A third technique, *Sales Potential Analysis*, has none of the drawbacks of the first two systems. It does not require daily inventory, but information can be almost current. This system is based on the actual sales mix and is therefore more realistic. Finally, it requires very little management time. It is estimated that the procedure can be accomplished in less than a half hour a day.

Requirements for "Sales Potential Analysis"

To set up a *Sales Potential Analysis* Beverage Control System, these are the requirements:

A. A standard price list and portion specifications for all drinks at the bar or serving unit.
B. Computation of the potential sales value of each bottle of liquor based on these data.
C. A supply, "par stock," for the serving unit sufficient to prevent running out during the serving period.
D. A requisition system to insure that the "par stock" is maintained, possibly by swapping empty bottles for full ones.
E. An analysis sheet with daily entries showing the sales potential of all stocks and the running totals of actual sales.

Regardless of what method is used, the important thing to keep in mind in boosting beverage profits is that you must know how much it costs to pour a drink and whether you are getting the full potential income from each bottle.

Hospitality, in the July, 1973, issue of its Restaurant edition (page R-41), suggests a Beverage Cost Control form along these lines:

BRAND	Bottle Size	Number Of Bottles Consumed	Cost Per Bottle	Total Beverage Cost	Estimated Number Of Drinks	Price Per Drink	Estimated Sales Value
CANADIAN CLUB	Fifth	4.0	$6.40	$25.60	80	$1.25	$100.00
OLD GRAND DAD	Fifth	2.4	6.00	14.40	48	1.25	60.00
BEEFEATERS GIN	Fifth	1.6	5.60	8.96	32	1.25	40.00
TOTAL LIQUOR				709.80			2600.00
TOTAL WINE				133.25			325.00
TOTAL BEER				123.75			375.00
SODA & MIXERS				37.60			—
TOTAL BEVERAGE COST AND SALES				1,004.40			3,300.00

Attainable Beverage Cost % =$1,004.40 ÷ 3,300.00 = 30.4%

Even Bartending Has Been Automated

There are also a number of electronic and mechanical devices and methods on the market designed to reduce liquor waste, discourage theft and improve profits. An electronic liquor dispensing system cuts bar costs by eliminating spillage and overpouring; provides a recorded sale for every drink poured direct from locked inventory. Selling from several hundred dollars to over $15,000, electronic dispensing systems are both accurate and efficient. It is reported that as many as seven drinks in 10 seconds can be dispensed by a quick-handed bartender.

Effecting Economies Through Payroll Control

As a service business, innkeeping has a heavy labor content. Significant economies can be realized through effective payroll control. One approach, of course, is to work constantly at methods improvement and to try to motivate employees to be more productive. Another is the application of modern technology such as Electronic Data Processing and Automation, to hotel operations wherever possible.

Ways in which labor cost savings can be made include the following:

1. Reduction in hours of service—opening dining room for lunch and dinner only, closing down room service after 11:00 P.M., etc..
2. Elimination of luxury type services, especially when not reflected in rates —many customers, it is thought, would make their own beds, for example, if this would enable them to save on their room rate.
3. Utilization of handicapped, senior citizens, part-time or temporary help, young people and disadvantaged wherever feasible for jobs within their capacity to perform well.
4. Work simplification—elimination of unnecessary or duplicating procedures and thorough analysis of operations from methods engineering standpoint.
5. Reduction in overtime payments by better scheduling and use of temporary or part-time help.
6. Improved recruitment, selection, orientation and training to obtain and retain qualified and motivated employees.
7. Supervision which sets clear and attainable objectives, assists in overcoming problems, and which requires a high standard of performance by employees.

Motel 6 Cost-Cutting Techniques

How the Motel 6 chain, an organization catering to budget-minded travelers, reduces costs is reported below:

"(1) One piece 'wipe clean' fiberglass shower stalls with rounded corners are installed to reduce bathroom cleaning time. (2) Lavatories are equipped with one, rather than two, faucets. This reduces repair costs. (3) Styrofoam drinking glasses are used because it is cheaper to throw them away than it is to wash regular glasses. (4) 'Maintenance teams,' which operate from the home office, visit each property periodically, at which time painting and routine repairs are taken care of. This means that only emergency repairs are made by local contractors. (5) A traveling housekeeper visits each property to teach maids the latest cleaning techniques and introduce them to new products. (6) All linen is washed in an on-premise laundry. This cuts cost of linen to 35¢ per room per day, half what the chain paid when it used linen services. (7) In most cases, the chain buys the best products available because they are more economical in the long run. This is said to be especially true of mattresses, hardware and appliances. (8) The company saves money by making mass purchases. It recently saved $7,000 by making a large purchase of Styrofoam cups. (9) A daily record is kept on how much time it takes maids to clean each room. If it takes more than 30 minutes, she is wasting time. If she takes less, she is not cleaning properly. This standardization of cleaning time is possible because all rooms are the same except some have two double beds while others have only one. (10) Only husband and wife teams are hired to manage the properties. In most cases, these are retired couples, including ex-military people, which means they select their managerial manpower from a source other employers systematically avoid."[1]

Essential Elements of Management Information

Successful planning, operation and control of a hotel/motel is dependent on accurate, timely and complete management information. The sources of this information include guest registration forms, guest charge vouchers, requisitions, purchase orders, bank checks, records of deposit, etc.; all records of original transactions.

In addition, there are the summary records—front office cash sheet, guest ledger transcript, payroll sheet, journals of various kinds and a general ledger as well as other records of transactions similar in nature.

These records are used to aid in preparing the balance sheet and income statement as well as other special reports management might require from time to time—room sales comparisons, costs of certain items, accounts receivable, etc..

An analysis of the information provided is an essential element in making decisions on budgeting, pricing, capital expenditures, advertising, financing and the like.

The setting up and operation of management records is a job best left to the experts, but they should satisfy these criteria:

1. Provide a complete and permanent record of all business transactions which is understandable, accurate, timely and reliable.
2. Include controls which will avoid losses through theft, embezzlement, error or ineptitude.
3. Furnish the data needed to optimize profits in useful form at a time when decisions are being made.

---

[1]Motel/Hotel "Insider" Newsletter, March 19, 1973, p. 2.

An invaluable aid in achieving these objectives is the *Uniform System of Accounts for Hotels* which is obtainable from the American Hotel & Motel Association, 888 Seventh Avenue, New York, N. Y. 10019. This document sets up a common financial denominator which facilitates comparison of operational and financial results among different properties.

Records Required by Federal Government

Speaking of records, the following are required by federal law:

Records of all alcoholic beverages received and sold with details. (Retain for two years.)

Records of wages paid, amounts paid to State unemployment funds, etc. (Retain for four years after due date of tax or date of payment.)

Employment records relative to wages, hours, sex, occupation, conditions of employment, etc. (Keep 2-3 years.)

Books and accounts in support of income tax returns and depreciation for income tax purposes. (Keep as long as needed for final determination of tax liability.)

Wage Retention Plan (sick pay) records showing dates of absence, rates of pay and records substantiating failure to withhold income tax (until final determination of tax liability).

Income tax withholding records of wages paid, tax withheld, statements to employees, etc. (Keep for four years after due date of tax or date of payment.)

Federal insurance contributions records of remuneration to each employee with supporting detail. (Retain four years after due date of tax or date of payment.)

Taxes Innkeepers Must Pay

A wide range of taxes apply to the accommodations business. In addition to federal income tax withholding from employees' pay and federal excise taxes if the property operates a shop selling merchandise subject to this tax, there are these federal taxes: Social Security jointly with employees, possibly self-employment Social Security tax, and unemployment tax.

State and local taxes include unemployment, personal income, corporation or business franchise, sales, room, real estate, personal property, and capital gains-dividend taxes.

Because of the complexity and frequent changes in tax laws, the services of a qualified tax accountant and lawyer should be sought in setting up tax records and preparing returns.

How to Use Depreciation to Save on Taxes

Depreciation is one of the largest expense items in operating a hotel/motel and can be a source of substantial tax savings. The three principal methods of computing depreciation are:

Straight-Line—Most commonly used, this method employs the cost or other basis of the property, less its estimated salvage, deducted in equal annual installments during its estimated useful life.

Declining Balance—Permits a faster write-off in early years. The greatest depreciation is taken in the first year with decreasing amounts in each succeeding year. Salvage value is not considered.

Sum-of-the-Years-Digit—Similar to the declining balance method, this approach multiplies a fraction to the cost or basis of the property, less its estimated salvage value. The numerator of the fraction for a given year is the number of remaining years of useful life of the property; the denominator is the *sum* of the numbers representing the total years of life of the property.

A new opportunity for tax savings through depreciation write-offs on furniture, fixtures and equipment—but not real estate—is provided by the *Asset Depreciation Range System.* Under this new system, more flexible "guidelines" or asset depreciation *ranges* are established which permit selection of a useful life for qualifying items appropriate to the type of operation and in line with previous experience. For example, an item which, prior to 1971, had a guideline life of 20 years could, at the option of the purchaser, now be written off over only 16 years or as many as 24. The faster write-off results, of course, in increased current deductions for depreciation. The only hitch in this new method is that, if selected, it must be used for *all* equipment purchased during the year.

Adequate Insurance Is Essential

Not only is the physical plant of a hotel/motel costly, but the possibility of litigation arising from personal injuries of guests and employees is great. For this reason, careful attention needs to be paid to protection of the investment through adequate insurance.

Depending on factors such as location, construction, equipment and type of business, insurance coverage which would be required or desirable might include all or most of the following:

Destruction, damage or theft of your own property

     a. Fire insurance
     b. Extended coverage (added to fire insurance policy)
        (1) Windstorm
        (2) Hail
        (3) Explosion
        (4) Riot and civil commotion
        (5) Falling aircraft
        (6) Damage by vehicles
        (7) Smoke
     c. Vandalism and malicious mischief (added to fire insurance policy)
     d. Sprinkler leakage
     e. Water damage

    f. Plate glass
    g. Flood and earthquake
    h. Boiler and machinery
    i. Automobile physical damage
    j. Fine arts
    k. Burglary and theft
    l. Fidelity (employee dishonesty)
    m. Surety and license bonds

Loss of income because of the interruption of your business

    a. Business interruption
    b. Rental value
    c. Extra expense

Exposure to financial loss because of claims against you as the result of injury to others or damage to others' property because of some activity for which you are responsible

    a. Comprehensive general liability
    b. Elevator liability
    c. Products liability
    d. Owners protective liability
    e. Personal liability
    f. Dram shop liability
    g. Automobile liability
      (1) Owned cars
      (2) Non-owned cars
      (3) Hired cars
    h. Garage keepers liability
    i. Umbrella excess

Injury, illness, retirement or death of management personnel or members of your staff

    a. Workmen's compensation
    b. Group insurance
      (1) Life and accidental death and dismemberment
      (2) Hospitalization
      (3) Surgical coverage
      (4) Major medical
      (5) Medicare supplement
      (6) Disability (accident and sickness)
      (7) Travel accident
    c. Key man life insurance
    d. Partnership life insurance
    e. Pensions
    f. Deferred compensation

Saving on Insurance

All of the coverages listed, except those dealing with employee or management injury, illness, retirement or death, are generally available in one package type known as a "multi-peril" policy. Such policies offer substantial savings over the cost of individual policies giving the same protection. Another advantage of package policies, aside from premiums which range from 10% to 30% lower than on conventional policies offering the same coverage, is that they simplify recordkeeping and accounting. Taking out a package policy means keeping track of only one expiration date and paying one premium instead of many.

Additional ways insurance costs can be held down include—

A. Shopping around to get the best coverage for your premium dollar.

B. Giving adequate consideration to promptness and fairness in settling your claims in choosing an insurance company.

C. Reviewing insurance coverage at least annually, not only to be sure it is adequate in an inflationary period, but also to eliminate unnecessary or excess coverage.

D. Getting reduced rates as a result of physical changes in the property which eliminate hazards, addition of fire-resistant materials and safeguards, and changes in type of occupancy.

E. Taking three or five-year policies instead of one year. Premium savings can be considerable.

Procedures to Reduce Bad Debts

Equally as important as conserving money is the need to avoid losing it outright. One insurance company estimates the total annual loss to business from theft is $10 billion. Embezzlement costs employers an estimated $3 billion a year. Employee theft costs $1 billion. Forgery costs $375 million. Customer stealing costs $500 million. Bad debt losses of the U. S. lodging industry are topping $30 million a year.

To help reduce bad debt losses at the front office, routine procedures should include the following:

(1) Determine at the time of registration whether the guest intends to use a credit card. (2) If so, ask to see the card and imprint it on a charge form "to speed up check-out." This will provide a later opportunity to check the card number against the cancellation list of the issuing company. At least one credit card company has a computerized system which provides almost instantaneous verification of card numbers dialed on a touch-tone telephone. (3) In any case, a record should be made of the company and card number on the guest folio. (4) Submit credit card charges promptly. (5) Instruct employees to be sure that they use the right ticket for the credit card proffered, that all copies are legible, that the guest signs the ticket.

How to Set Up Your Own Retirement Program

If you are the owner-operator of a hotel or motel, you shouldn't overlook the retirement income opportunity available to you under the Keogh Act. This federal legislation enables those who are their own bosses to set aside retirement dollars and receive current income tax deductions. It also allows the retirement fund to further expand by permitting interest or reinvested dividends to be free of any tax liability during the individual's working years.

Under the Act, a self-employed person may contribute up to 15 percent of his annual earnings or $7,500—whichever is less—to an approved retirement program. There are five methods which may be used to satisfy the investment requirements of the Keogh Act:

1. Through a trust with a bank acting as trustee.
2. Through the purchase of life insurance, or annuity contracts from an insurance company.
3. Through the purchase of special U. S. Government bonds.
4. Through face-amount certificates purchased from an investment company.
5. Through the purchase of open-end mutual fund shares with a bank as custodian.

Any full time employee (working more than 20 hours a week and more than five months a year) must be included in the plan. An employee can be included any time within the first three years of his employment depending on how the plan is set up. The employer must contribute for all eligible employees, at least the same percentage of earned income as he contributes for himself. For example: If one earns $45,000 a year, the maximum contribution he can make for himself on a deduction-from-income basis is $6,750. This is 15% of earnings. Hence, the amount of the employer's contribution for his employees would be 15% of the employee's net income. It is important to note that a self-employed individual also qualifies under the Keogh plan if he does not employ *anyone.*

Another pertinent feature of the plan, if there are participants other than the owner of the business, is the option of contributing up to *another* 10% of earned income up to $2,500 as a voluntary addition to one's retirement fund. This additional voluntary contribution is not deductible for tax purposes, but income earned by the fund compounds on a currently tax-free basis.

Under the Keogh plan, withdrawals may be made beginning at age 59½ and must commence no later than age 70½.

Recent liberalization of the Keogh Act sets up an entirely new classification of pensions for those who are not self-employed, but do not qualify for pensions where they work. Called Individual Retirement Accounts, they permit tax-free contributions of 15% of income or $1,500 a year.

How to Win the "Numbers Game"

Improving the profitability of a going operation, or planning for profits in a new hotel/motel venture, requires attention to six major factors—

Sales—sources of income
Scheduling—efficient use of personnel
Maintenance—keeping property modern and in good operating condition
Expense Control—holding down minor costs
Purchasing—getting the right products at the right prices
Pricing—setting rates that are competitive yet profitable

Considering the fact that the profit margin in the average property is only about five percent of sales, it is obvious that inattention to any one of these factors can cause profits to plummet or disappear entirely.

Get a Good Accountant!

Undoubtedly the best single bit of advice which can be offered to the reader in the whole area of financial management is: Get yourself the best accountant you can find —and *pay attention to him!* In accounting, as elsewhere, "a little knowledge can be a dangerous thing." For this reason, the various aspects of accounting as they pertain to the innkeeping business are best left to the experts.

Helpful as a good accountant may be in keeping or helping to put a hotel/motel "in the black," there is little he can do to offset mistakes in original financing. It has been said, perceptively, that how a property is financed often makes the difference between profitable operation and mounting losses.

Hotel/Motel Financing Is a New "Ball Game"

There have been great changes in hotel/motel financing in recent years. The general pattern until recently had been for ownership to obtain a first mortgage from a life insurance company, pension fund or a bank. These were fixed loans at fixed interest rates repayable in from 15 to 25 years. In addition to the first mortgage, secondary financing might include a subordinated ground lease, a second mortgage or an equipment lease. Under these conditions, it was frequently the case that between 90 percent and 100 percent of the actual cost of the property was financed requiring very little capital investment on the part of the owner.

The newer type of borrowing situation finds many institutional lenders demanding higher returns—what else?—and a "piece of the action." In some cases it is a percentage of gross, in others a percentage of profit.

Non-traditional Sources of Funds

As a way around these demands, other sources of capital have been sought out by hotel/motel owners. One alternative which has become increasingly popular is the *joint venture* or *partnership agreement*. Under this type of arrangement, the hotel/motel company or operator puts up 50 percent of the required capital and the remainder is supplied by an industrial concern, a national chain, an insurance company, conglomerate or whatever. The hotel company operator is employed as *management agent* for the partnership. Typical of this type of joint venture: the Western International's Century Plaza Hotel in Los Angeles, an undertaking in cooperation with ALCOA.

Sale-leaseback is still another method of financing a property when additional funds are needed. It enables the original owner to secure a sizable amount of cash for expansion or other purposes while still retaining control of the business. The procedure transfers ownership without changing management. It is suggested that maximum institutional first mortgage financing be obtained before negotiating a sale-leaseback since this will permit the operator to obtain a lower average annual rental.

Syndication Financing

Offering a number of advantages over mortgage loans is financing by syndication. Among them are these:

1. Syndication capital can be obtained at lower interest rates.

2. There is a large and eager market because of tax shelter and capital gains benefits offered by syndication.

3. Payments need not be paid to investors until justified by earnings in contrast to a mortgage loan that would require monthly payments irrespective of earnings.

Among hotel/motel organizations involved in syndication financing is Sheraton Motor Inns which is managing a number of properties owned by syndication investors.

In setting up a syndicate to own a hotel/motel it is essential that the projected return be adequate to (1) attract investors, (2) cover syndication costs, and (3) provide a "cushion" for contingencies.

A variety of formats is available. Included are general or limited partnerships—with or without leaseback—"going public" by forming a corporation, joint venture and others.

Should the lease-back route be decided upon, consideration needs to be given to questions such as:

1. What rent shall be paid to the investor?
2. When do payments start?
3. Will the lease be guaranteed for a definite period of time?

Advantages of "Going Public"

Just as there are a number of companies with annual sales of well over $100 million that are privately held, there are small hotel companies that are publicly owned. Aside from being in vogue, "going public" has several advantages which an independent hotel owner might want to consider. Probably the most important is that it is a good source of funds for expansion or improvement. Another advantage is that it enables the company to offer stock options as an incentive to attract high calibre management and to reward capable employees. Public ownership affords an opportunity to retain control of a company without having to make a total financial commitment to it. It also aids expansion through the issuance of securities instead of cash payments.

By "going public" a hotel owner can facilitate his retirement from the business and, at the same time, contribute to a more orderly and less expensive settling of his estate when he dies.

There are, of course, some disadvantages which should not be lost sight of—less independence of action in running the business is the major one—so a careful weighing of the pros and cons with the advice of an attorney and an accountant are "musts." For more information, see *A Complete Guide to Making A Public Stock Offering* by Winter and *Going Public: A Practical Handbook of Procedures and Forms* by Berman, Prentice-Hall, Inc.

Sheraton's Use of Leverage

A classic example of astute financing is the building of the Sheraton Hotels chain by the late Ernest Henderson from four hotels in 1941 to 92 hotels and 104 motor inns in the mid-sixties–all through acquisition, management-lease and franchise.

Explaining how his father used "leverage" to stretch his cash, Ernest Henderson III gave students at the University of Massachusetts this illustration:

Suppose Mr. Henderson was seeking to obtain a property generating $100,000 annual income with a minimum of cash. Half of the offering price of $800,000 could be borrowed from a lending institution at six percent. If the owner would take a second mortgage for $500,000, the offering price could be increased to a million dollars if necessary. With a $400,000 first mortgage and a $500,000 second mortgage, the cash outlay required of Sheraton would be only $100,000.

Condominiums Can Also Generate Funds

In resort areas, particularly still another "twist" in financing is being used. Apartments with two or three bedrooms are sold, while still on the drawing board, as condominiums. Purchasers agree, through a sale-leaseback contract, to use their apartments for only a few weeks a year and to let the operator rent the rooms for the remainder of the time. Funds raised in this fashion are available to pay off the rented building or to finance a new project.

The condominium approach to financing is in wide-spread use in places such as Spain's Costa del Sol and Majorca as well as in Florida. In the Miami area, particularly, a number of hotels unable to keep up with the competition on a transient trade basis have sought refuge in condominium arrangements.

How to Cut Financing Costs

1. Consider leasing out restaurant and bar to an independent operator.
2. If possible, try to get a "subordination" clause in the ground lease or purchase contract if land is not purchased outright for cash. In either case, you can borrow against the land as well as the building and both primary and secondary financing are easier to arrange.
3. Try to get the lender to extend the construction loan or waive amortization payments during the first six to 12 months of operation when income is likely to be low.
4. Ask for prepayment privileges so, if things go well, you can refinance to reduce carrying charges or provide capital for expansion or modernization.

Government Financial Aid Available

In many cases, financing can be obtained from federal government sources as well as the financial community. The Small Business Administration makes loans to qualifying hotels and motels unable to borrow on reasonable terms from private lending sources. SBA loans may be made to lodging establishments for construction, conversion or expansion; for purchase of facilities, equipment and supplies, and for working capital.

A hotel or motel that is independently owned and operated, not dominant in its field, and that meets current criteria as to number of employees, assets, net income and credit standing, should qualify for SBA financial assistance.

Another source of federal financial aid is the Economic Development Administration set up to assist in the economic development of distressed areas. To encourage private investment in such areas, the EDA will make low-interest, long-term loans for the purchase or development of land and facilities including construction of new hotels and motels as well as alteration, conversion or expansion of existing properties. It also will guarantee a large part of working capital loans made to private borrowers by private lending institutions under specified conditions.

Considerations in Negotiating a Management Contract

Management contracts and leasing are gaining in popularity as ways to facilitate expansion because they offer a hotel corporation limited long-term debt, low depreciation and high after-tax earnings.

In negotiating a management contract, the following 25 points should be covered, according to Stephen W. Brener, Senior Vice-President, Helmsley-Spear:

1. The management agent must be employed as the exclusive operator of the property.
2. The owner must state that all expenses are his and that he is responsible for advancing all funds. The maximum amount of individual items of expense that do not require review and approval of the owner must be stated, so that agent can know limits within which he can contract.
3. Agent must submit an estimate of operating capital. Owner deposits same into a bank account upon which only agent can withdraw. After opening, agent remits excess dollars monthly to owner.
4. There should be a section stating who will pay and the method of paying all non-operating expenses, plus one covering maximum amount of capital expenses that can be incurred without owner's prior consent.
5. Agreement must include detailed budget and policy clause allowing the owner and his consultant the right to review and recommend.
6. Agent is responsible for maintaining books and records and these must be accessible to owner or his representative.
7. Agent must furnish detailed daily and other reports such as payroll, forecasts, city ledger analysis, and so forth, to owner and his consultant. In addition, provision must be made for a year-end certified statement.
8. A fixed maximum percentage of gross sales applicable to sales promotion must be agreed upon. Ninety days prior to a fiscal year, a detailed breakdown of advertising must be submitted.
9. A stated fund for replacements, which can be cumulative, must be included in the agreement.
10. Defining the fixed percentage of gross sales for repairs and maintenance is also a necessity.
11. Owner must agree to provide all necessary insurance.
12. The agreement must contain a fire clause as well as a condemnation clause.

13. Both parties must agree to work together to create suitable plans and specifications.

14. Agent must advise on type, quality, quantity, layout, and design of furniture, fixtures, equipment, supplies and all start-up inventories. Agent is responsible for preparing detailed lists and budgets for same.

15. Agent must agree to properly and efficiently open and operate the business as soon as it is ready.

16. Agent must agree to train personnel and do promotion work prior to opening, and must provide owner with detailed budget for the pre-opening and opening expenses.

17. Agent is solely responsible for hiring and discharging all help.

18. Agent agrees to negotiate all leases for stores, offices and lobby or, if owner wishes, to work with owner and owner's local real estate representative to accomplish this.

19. Agent agrees to provide supervisory services of all its executive and special departments.

20. A fixed basis for payment of management fee is spelled out explicitly in the contract.

21. A cancellation clause is usually included.

22. All terms of the agreement and renewals thereof are clearly stipulated.

23. If agent is a chain or franchise organization, definition of the area of competition is important for both parties and must be stated in the agreement.

24. Agent when executing the agreement will be expected to guarantee its performance.

25. A section entitled "Definitions" is always built into a management agreement, for items such as fiscal year, gross income, operating profit, and so forth must all be fully explained.[1]

If You Lease . . .

While leasing is an accepted method of acquiring the operation of a hotel/motel, there are some pitfalls involved. It is well to secure the advice of a hospitality consultant or a lawyer experienced in such matters before entering into a lease agreement.

A hotel/motel lease is usually a long-term arrangement between landlord and tenant. From the operator's point of view, the minimum term of the lease should be 15 years, much longer if possible. Often, leases are for 50 to 99 years divided into set periods of anywhere from 15 to 25 years. Since most leases provide for minimum rentals plus percentage agreements, long-term lease agreements permit landlords an increased rate of return to compensate for inflation. On the other hand, they provide the tenant with a valuable estate which can be sold, financed and used as a basis for expanding in the industry.

Properly drawn, a lease offers protection to both landlord and tenant while making it

---

[1]Stephen Brener, "Management Contract," *Resort Management*, February 1965, p. 30.

possible to acquire operation of a property with considerably less investment—both initial equity (down payment) and long-term obligation (mortgage)—than purchase.

Problems in Pricing

One of the knottiest problems a hotelier must face is that of developing a viable pricing policy. He has to establish room rates which are competitive if he is to keep occupancy at a satisfactory level. And at the same time his rates must be such as to provide a fair profit under average occupancy conditions. Gone by the boards in these inflationary days is the old rule-of-thumb: a dollar a day of average rate per occupied room for every $1,000 of total cost. With total costs of some new properties reaching above $50,000 a room, room rates would have to be unconscionably high just to break even, let alone show a small profit.

Complicating the pricing problem is the pressure some companies are capable of exerting in order to get preferential rates for the large numbers of their people who travel frequently. By persuading cooperating hotels and motels to offer their personnel "guaranteed rates," these companies assure that their representatives will only have to pay a pre-set low rate, usually at or just above the minimum of the hotel or motel. Even if moderately priced rooms are no longer available when the guest checks in, and he has to be assigned a luxurious suite, he still pays only the low guaranteed rate. In some cases, companies responsible for a large volume of business have negotiated guaranteed rates for their personnel well below the minimum charged the public. Hilton Hotels Corp. has guaranteed rate arrangements in effect with several thousand companies and companies such as Ford list almost 1,000 U.S. and foreign establishments offering guaranteed rates to Ford employees.

There seems little question that offering guaranteed rates to good customers helps keep occupancy up. Further, proponents of the plan point out, the most expensive accommodations are usually the last to be sold and might otherwise be empty if not assigned to a guaranteed rate guest.

Out and out price gouging and, at the other extreme, rate cutting are evils equally deplored by most sophisticated hoteliers, hotel accounting firms and lodging industry trade associations. To some extent, supply and demand does, and should, exert an influence on rates. No one should question a hotel's right to charge premium rates at the height of the resort season or during Mardi Gras week in New Orleans, for example. Likewise, there should be no quarrel with offering promotional rates in the off-season. Competition also must be factored in when rates are set since it is economically suicidal to charge well above the prices neighboring properties are getting for comparable accommodations.

But the most important single consideration in establishing a hotel's or motel's rates must be the costs which have to be met in running the operation. Provision for a margin of profit is also essential.

Rate Cutting Is A Losing Proposition

While a temporary advantage may be gained by cutting rates further than justified by decreases in costs, in the long run the practice will usually result in cut-throat competition ending up with all properties involved losing money.

Along the same line, sad experience has proven many times over that a hotel can't long continue giving customers "something for nothing" and stay out of the red. Costly menu substitutions, extra facilities and services, etc., asked for by guests must be charged for at the going rate.

Rate cutting of even modest dimensions can be extremely harmful to a property's profit and loss statement. With a normal occupancy of 70 percent, for example, a reduction of only five percent in room rates would require a 75 percent occupancy at the lower rate to provide the same income; a 10 percent reduction in rate would require more than 80 percent occupancy.

Put another way, take a 100 room motel with a single room rate of $15 a day. If 70 percent of the rooms are sold at this rate, the day's revenue is $1,050. On the other hand, if a "commercial" rate of $12 a day is offered and occupancy is increased to 80 percent, the daily revenue is only $960. This adds up to a revenue loss of $90 a day, nearly $33,000 a year.

Furthermore, this does not take into account the cost of servicing the additional rooms sold, approximately $40 a day, nearly $15,000 a year. Taking the lost revenue and increased costs together, this seemingly harmless "merchandising" could cost this small property something in the order of $50,000 annually, a substantial sum indeed.

Prescription to Prevent Rate Cutting

The late Allan C. George, a partner of Harris, Kerr, Forster and Co., offered this still appropriate advice:

1. Establish a price structure that will gain guest acceptance for the type and quality of the services furnished and yield a reasonable profit at a normal average volume of business.
2. Be sure that prices established are in fair relationship with those of other hotels in its general competitive class.
3. Do not engage in the practice of offering conventions or groups free guest rooms, meeting rooms, or exhibit space or underquote to them on banquets, meals, or receptions.
4. Seek out constructive and legitimate ways to develop new business such as package tours, while avoiding any schemes which simply divert existing business from other hotels with benefit accruing only to the bargain-hunting guest.
5. Work to establish mutual understanding among innkeepers in competitive areas of the harmful results to everyone from rate cutting.
6. Sustain rates through improved salesmanship and services.

The Hubbart Formula

A time-proven method for evaluating hotel room rate structure is the Hubbart Formula developed in the late forties under the aegis of the America Hotel & Motel

Association. Designed to establish rates which will be adequate to cover operating costs and provide a reasonable return on the fair value of the property, the Hubbart Formula has been applied with good results by residential and transient hotels as well as resorts.

The first step in applying the Hubbart Formula is to determine the total room sales volume needed to cover costs and expected profit. To get this figure, annual operating expenses; taxes, insurance, etc.; depreciation on buildings, furniture, fixtures and equipment; and expected return on investment are totalled. Then credits from sources other than rooms (income from store rentals, credit from store rentals, food and beverage operations and miscellaneous income) are deducted. The resulting figure is the amount which room sales must provide to cover operating expenses and profit.

The second step is to compute the average daily rate per occupied room needed to cover costs and a reasonable profit. To arrive at this figure, multiply number of guest rooms available for rental by 365. Then deduct from this an estimated percentage for average vacancies. This will give the number of rooms to be occupied at estimated average occupancy.

The total room sales amount to cover costs and profit is then divided by the estimated number of occupied rooms to obtain the required average rate per occupied room.

Copies of the Hubbart Formula giving specific examples are available from AH&MA.

The Roth Room Pricing Program

Another room pricing method, developed by Elmer Roth Management Associates, is said to produce maximum revenue at all levels of occupancy while, at the same time, assuring a high degree of guest satisfaction. The Roth room pricing program enables the innkeeper to determine:

1. A price for each room that reflects its true value in relation to all other rooms.
2. The correct number of rooms at each rate to satisfy the demand for rooms at that rate.
3. Where money for upgrading and refurbishing should be spent to insure the greatest return.

In one example cited by Mr. Roth, the great bulk of rooms in a particular hotel had the same rate. While there were some very high priced accommodations, there were only a few rooms available in the lower rate range where a substantial demand existed. Too many rooms were priced at the minimum rate although they could have commanded a higher price.

Application of the Roth formula resulted in an increase in income of an estimated $57,000 annually.

Four Steps to Profitable Pricing

While the procedures of the Roth plan are detailed, although not complicated, the steps that it prescribes are these:

1. Analyze the demand for rooms on average days to determine percentage of guests paying each rate.
2. Compare supply and demand by applying obtained percentages to available rooms. This will tell how many rooms should be provided at each rate to satisfy demand exactly.
3. Evaluate all rooms to establish proper value relationship among them by identifying physical attributes making one room more desirable than another. Compare the number of room classifications obtained by this procedure with number of rates in existing rate structure. They should be equal. If not, there are inequities in the rate structure.
4. Establish new rate structure that will provide the closest match between the demand for rooms at given rates and available rooms at those rates.

Biting the Bullet

While it may not be pleasant to contemplate, it is possible that the property you are operating or own is going downhill in more ways than one. Very likely an analysis of your pricing policy will reveal this fact. What to do?

Some years ago, the Ways and Means Committee of AH&MA developed a Diagnosis Kit which offered these suggestions to distressed and distraught hoteliers:

"1. If you're losing money and you are below the average occupancy percentage for your city or area, get out of the business.
"2. If the market is declining and the new competition is increasing, get out of the business.
"3. If you're in doubt about continuing in business, and if you can sell at *any* profit, *sell* and get out of the business.
"4. If you have an opportunity to lease, make a deal, preferably net. If you can receive a rental which covers your mortgage payments and gives you a better return on your equity than you can normally make elsewhere, by all means make it."

On the other hand . . .

"If the city occupancy is over 60 percent and the market is increasing, consider improving the facilities with a complete renovation program, provided—

(a) You have a choice location
(b) Basic facilities can be made competitive or superior to competition.
(c) You can pay for a complete renovation
(d) Realistic forecast shows adequate earnings to pay for financing."

Conversion Might Be the Answer

There is still another possibility to be considered if the facts show it would be unprofitable to remain in the innkeeping business and sale or leasing opportunities are not immediately at hand. In this case, serious thought might be given to conversion of the hotel/motel to one of the following types of facilities:

Medical/Dental Clinic	Senior Citizen Housing
Private Club/Fraternal Lodge	Stores/Shopping Center
Student/Faculty Housing	School/College Classrooms
Hospital/Nursing Home	Hospital Staff Housing
Religious Seminary/Convent	Apartments/Co-Op/Condominium
Residence Club	Offices
Manufacturing Facility	Warehouse
Municipal Building	Trade School
Private School	Parking Structure/Garage

Stretching Your Purchasing Dollar

The reverse side of the pricing coin is cost control. One of the best ways to help control costs is through the utilization of up-to-date purchasing techniques and procedures. In making purchasing decisions, consideration needs to be given to Quality, Service, and Price. All are important although, depending on circumstances, one or the other may be paramount at any given time.

A sound purchasing program will insure that the hotel/motel obtains the right products in the right quantity and quality at the right time and price. In so doing, it can substantially reduce investment and operating costs through reduced spoilage, pilferage and obsolescence.

Because of the absence of effective management control in decentralized purchasing—with each department making its own purchases—it is seldom found in the lodging industry.

Centralized purchasing, with a single person or department in charge of all purchasing, on the other hand, gives good control over expenditures and results in substantially lower costs overall.

Guidelines for Buying Wisely and Well

1. Plan and schedule purchases. Avoid impulse buying.
2. Establish and purchase by specifications.
3. Research the market to keep abreast of new products, new supplies.
4. Follow up on orders to insure prompt delivery.
5. Check deliveries to be sure merchandise is exactly as ordered and that invoices are accurate.
6. Keep accurate and complete purchase records.
7. Salvage all usable material such as used soap, torn sheets, etc..
8. Stick to purchasing budget to reduce waste.

9. Encourage all employees to practice economy and avoid waste, to suggest ways to cut costs and improve efficiency.
10. Take advantage of quantity or bulk discounts. But don't buy more than can be used in a reasonable period of time.
11. Avail yourself of discounts for paying cash.
12. Look for sales, promotional offers and seasonal "buys" to get the most for your dollars.
13. Shop first among companies specializing in serving the hospitality industry such as contract furnishers.
14. In purchasing services—painting, plumbing, etc.—don't go bargain hunting. This is one area where it pays to emphasize reliability and competence rather than price alone.

Going The Leasing Route

Often, especially when working capital is low, it pays to consider leasing equipment and furnishings. Among the advantages of leasing over purchasing are:

1. Capital is not tied up.
2. Service and warranty obligations are more likely to be honored without a hassle.
3. Nearly always, a favorable lease-purchase arrangement is available in case the hotel/motel operator opts in favor of purchase at a later date.

While the leasing of TV sets, air conditioners, etc., has been common in the lodging industry for some time, there are several new developments. One, the leasing of telephone systems other than the locally-provided service, has resulted in savings of up to 25 percent on monthly telephone costs in a number of cases.

Another break-through has been leasing arrangements offering a complete package of room furnishings including such items as draperies, furniture, TV, and carpet from a single vendor.

A system of this type offered by one supplier allows a hotel/motel operator to lease any one or all of the following products for up to five years: furniture, case pieces, carpet, bedding, draperies, spreads, TV, electronic control system, message and master antenna systems, and air conditioners.

Hotel/Motel Managers
and the Law

Above all, today's successful innkeeper must be a business man. Like other businessmen, it is incumbent upon him to be cognizant of fields of specialization other than his own, but which have a direct bearing on his enterprise. One of these areas is the law.

Not only does a contemporary hotel manager need to know in broad terms his legal obligations to a guest, but he should be aware of his legal rights in respect to the guest's responsibilities to the hotel. Not to be knowledgeable in both could lead to loss of face, business, property and money.

As an innkeeper, the hotelman is concerned with the law as it relates to both buyers and sellers, landlord and tenant, unions and employees. He is also intimately involved with laws dealing with civil rights, liability and contracts as well as many other conditions and relationships.

He is subject to federal and state laws and local ordinances of a general nature as well as those applying specifically to hotels.

This chapter covers some of the more basic aspects of hotel law in order that the reader may better understand the general rights conferred and obligations imposed on innkeepers by the law.

Special laws relating to innkeeping as they apply in this country trace back to 14th century England. It is on the precedents established then and judicial opinions since, that the common law relating to hotels is based. Statute laws are those enacted by legislative bodies at the federal, state or local level.

Some of the legal questions with which an innkeeper should be familiar are: What is an inn? Who is a guest? What are the duties and liabilities of the innkeeper and what protections are afforded the innkeeper by the law?

An early, 1820, legal interpretation of what an inn is stated that an inn is "a house, the owner of which holds out that he will receive all travelers and sojourners who are willing to pay a price adequate to the sort of accommodation provided, and who come in a situation in which they are fit to be received."

In the eyes of most courts today, there is no legal difference between hotels and motels since both offer essentially the same facilities and services.

Some Important Legal Distinctions

There is, however, an important legal distinction between a motel/hotel and a boarding or rooming house. The latter do not qualify as hotels because "they do not minister to any absolute public necessity." Further, while an innkeeper may not arbitrarily accept or reject guests, a boardinghouse keeper is at liberty to deal with his customers on an individual basis, accepting or rejecting them at will. In addition, an innkeeper is under constraint not to vary the terms of his acceptance of a guest, while the boardinghouse keeper may make whatever arrangements he wishes with each guest on room rate, length of stay, etc., subject, of course, to anti-discrimination laws.

Hotels may at once be a hotel for transients and an apartment house for permanent guests. Some large city hotels in recent years have become cooperatives in which a small number of rooms have been set aside for transient guests. The law defines an apartment house as a group of units in a single building, each separate from the other, and arranged for independent housekeeping. Tenants have the right to exclusive possession of the occupied unit until the expiration or breach of the lease. Even though certain services and utilities are furnished, the relationship between the property and the occupants is that of landlord/tenant rather than innkeeper/guest even if no housekeeping is done in the apartments.

Even though several motel companies have entered the campground or trailer camp business there is a substantial body of legal opinion that holds that accommodations of this type are of a "casual" nature and do not give rise to the innkeeper/guest relationship.

While the law holds the owner of a property legally responsible for what takes place there, it is the manager who should be familiar enough with the law to avoid suits against him. The manager also should see to it that each employee is familiar with those laws that impinge directly on his job.

Not Every Occupant Is a Guest

Everyone using the facilities of a hotel is not necessarily a guest. The law separates patrons into two categories—invitees and licensees.

Invitees include registered guests, those visiting guests and patrons of restaurants, and bars on the premises. Policemen and firemen, as well as others entitled by law to enter the hotel, are considered invitees.

A licensee, on the other hand, is one who, while not specifically invited or especially welcomed, may be allowed to enter the property. This category would include a newsboy, a solicitor for a charity or someone coming in off the street to use a washroom. The express or implicit permission to enter a portion of the property is not without limits and the person who may venture beyond the area involved becomes a trespasser.

The Innkeeper-Guest Relationship

The innkeeper/guest relationship is established when the following conditions obtain:

1. The person is a *transient* coming from or returning to his home.
2. A "contract" exists between the innkeeper and the person based on their consent, expressed or implied, to the relationship.
3. An *agreement to pay* is in effect.

A person using a hotel for an illegal purpose, as well as someone sharing a guest's room without the knowledge or consent of the hotel, forfeits the rights he might have been entitled to under the innkeeper/guest relationship.

While it is generally believed that a person does not become a guest of a hotel until he registers, the fact is that the innkeeper/guest relationship can be and is established when each of the parties shows the *intent* to establish this relationship. This intent can be established by making a reservation. It is also not necessary that a specific room be assigned in order for the innkeeper/guest relationship to be established. If a person's luggage were stolen while he was waiting in line to register, for example, the hotel would have the same liability as if he had already registered and been assigned a room.

As a general rule, once the guest checks out and leaves the hotel, the guest/innkeeper relationship is terminated. The courts, however, seem to hold that the relationship may continue in effect for a "reasonable time" after the guest leaves to allow him to arrange for removal of luggage left at the hotel.

A not uncommon problem which innkeepers must face is what to do when guests extend their stay beyond the period for which they made reservations and this results in the inability to accommodate incoming guests with reservations. Situations such as this arise when resorts experience a spell of unpleasant weather or when transportation strikes, postponed events, etc. force guests to change their plans for departure. Although most innkeepers seem to prefer to allow the incumbent guest to extend his stay beyond the reserved period, from a strictly legal point of view the innkeeper is under no such obligation. At the end of the reserved period, the innkeeper/guest relationship expires and the guest becomes a trespasser if he attempts to remain without the innkeeper's consent. He is subject to forcible eviction if there is no more space available for incoming guests.

When You Can Refuse Accommodations

There are a number of reasons why accommodations legally may be refused:

1. Obviously, if none are available.

2. If the innkeeper has reason to believe the prospective guest might create a disturbance—intoxication or irrational actions.
3. If the prospective guest is a known criminal or his luggage contains something not permitted such as a gun.
4. If the prospective guest refuses to make advance payment or asks for lower rates, he may be turned away.

On the other hand, a prospective guest may not be refused accommodations based on age alone. Nor, of course, can an innkeeper refuse to accept a prospective guest because of race, color or creed since the passage of the Federal Civil Rights Act of 1964.

A hotel can refuse admittance to a visitor of a guest for the same reasons it can refuse to accommodate the guest. It can likewise evict guests or their visitors for the same reasons they might be refused admittance.

The right of eviction should be used with extreme caution if damage suits and unfavorable publicity are to be avoided. A hotel cannot legally evict a guest if in so doing it violates any of his rights or if the eviction would expose the guest to an unreasonable risk of harm.

In addition to his legal responsibility to accept prospective guests unless he has a legal reason for refusing admission, an innkeeper is legally responsible for protecting his guests and caring for their property.

Liability for Person

The hotel's liability for protecting guests from harm embraces the following:

1. Protection against danger caused by the defective condition of equipment or the premises—the building itself, walks, driveways, swimming pool, etc..
2. Protection against the carelessness of employees.
3. Against improper language or discourtesy of employees.
4. Against defamation of character or invasion of privacy.
5. Against physical harm caused by other guests.
6. Against the serving of unwholesome or poisonous food.

Liability for Property

An innkeeper's liability for a guest's property usually is contingent on two conditions: (1) that at the time of the loss the innkeeper/guest relationship existed and (2) that the property was under the administrative control of the innkeeper.

While hotels are generally liable for a guest's property entrusted to their care and where these conditions exist, the liability is limited if loss or damage to the property is caused by "an act of God, the public enemy or the guest's own negligence." An "act of God" could be a torrential rain, tornado or lightning—occurrences over which man has no control. The term "public enemy" refers to actions during a civil disturbance or by enemy soldiers in wartime. Contributory negligence results from the failure of the guest to exercise appropriate prudence with regard to the safeguarding of his own possessions.

Additional exceptions to strict liability arise from (1) acts of public authority such as police, (2) the inherent nature of the property which may lead to spoilage, (3) a fire not caused by the hotel.

Many states have laws which limit the innkeeper's liability for guests' property, but it is required that notices of statutory limitations be posted on the premises.

In the case of a guest's valuables stored in a hotel safe, liability is generally limited. It is necessary in most states that the guest be informed of the limitation which is in effect in the particular state in which the property is located.

Where guests choose to retain their valuables instead of depositing them in the hotel safe, unless state law provides differently, this is not considered negligence and does not relieve the hotel of liability.

Many hotels and motels leave notices in guest rooms advising patrons of measures available for protection of their property and person. A typical flyer of this type is reproduced here.

A Reminder—To Our Guests

The recent problems that some large urban hotels have experienced prompts this reminder of the facilities available at the Chase-Park Plaza for your protection and convenience.

SAFETY DEPOSIT VAULTS are provided without charge at the Front Office Cashiers counter. You are earnestly requested not to leave money, jewelry or valuables in your room as Missouri state laws absolve the hotel from liability for loss unless valuables are placed in a safe deposit box.

DOUBLE LOCKS AND CHAINS are provided on the inside of each guest room. Before retiring the bolt should be turned to secure the added lock insuring no disturbance and also secure the chain lock and do not release to open until you have identified the person that may request entrance.

HANDICAPPED PERSONS should at the time of registration or by calling the Assistant Manager on duty notify the Front Desk of any special problem they may have. Special note for emergency attention will be made of any sight, hearing, cast or use of crutches.

ROOM ACCOUNTS are payable upon departure unless a credit card has been issued or credit established. In addition to the Chase-Park Plaza credit card we also honor American Express, Diners, Master Charge, and guests desiring other arrangements should see the Credit Manager in the Executive Suite as soon as possible to avoid any inconvenience upon departure.

The Management
Chase-Park Plaza Hotel
St. Louis, Missouri

The Innkeeper's Lien

Traditionally when a guest failed to pay for accommodations provided and services rendered, the innkeeper could put a lien on his personal belongings. A lien is a claim on someone's property as security for payment of money due. Liens, in general, were allowed to be put on all guest baggage and, unless excluded by state law, on the automobile of the guest.

Once a lien was put on a guest's property, the hotel was required to exercise "reasonable care" of the property and might be liable for negligence if it failed to do so.

The question of innkeeper's liens may become academic in the near future if a state court decision declaring the California Innkeeper's Lien Law invalid is upheld in higher courts. More recently, the New York State Court of Appeals called that state's 100-year-old innkeeper's lien law unconstitutional. The New York court said:

"The innkeeper's right under lien law to seize a defaulting guest's property and to sell it at public auction is not questioned. All that is necessary is that the fundamentals of due process be observed."

By due process, the court said the guest should receive notice and a chance to be heard before the property seizure.

Obviously, the best way to prevent default on bills is to require advance payment. Failing that, an innkeeper could obtain a temporary injunction to restrain a guest from moving personal belongings.

The law on innkeeper's liens is very much in a state of flux and will bear close watching by hotelmen until the question is finally resolved.

Be on Guard Against Other Credit Losses

Many states have statutes that make it a criminal offense to defraud the proprietor of a hotel or motel by obtaining food or lodging without intending to pay for it or obtaining credit under false pretenses.

Innkeepers need to pay particular attention to their check cashing practices and verification of credit card ownership and expiration date if they are to avoid credit losses.

Check Cashing Tips

Experienced hotelmen pass along these suggestions for tripping up bad check passers and skippers:

*Require positive identification. Remember, even printed and government checks can be forgeries. They also may have been stolen and then forged. Since credentials such as driver's licenses, credit cards, etc., can be cancelled, lost, forged or stolen, make sure that the endorsement on the check corresponds to the payee's name. Also note if passer resembles photo on driver's license or other identification card.

*Insist that checks be endorsed in your presence while holding the identification card. This prevents the passer from copying the signature from the card, which may have been lost, stolen or forged.

*Start stalling if you become suspicious; call the bank if possible. When you stall, a suspect usually will leave in a hurry, often leaving the check behind.

*Warn your employees that bad check passers are particularly active over weekends, on holidays and during the summer vacation months.

*Look twice before cashing a rubber-stamped check.

*Question alterations. Remember, the payee's name can be altered; amounts raised and dates changed.

*Record all identification data before cashing checks. This can be noted on back or face of check.

*Try to obtain multiple identification.

*Try to get the license plate number of casher's car; this provides a better identification than an operator's license. In copying license data, be sure to include state and numbers, note whether owner's description matches that of passer and if signature is identical.

*Be cautious if the check offered is for more than the amount of the bill.

*Don't allow yourself to be hurried. Bad check passers try to work fast; you should take your time.

*Don't accept a Social Security card as identification; it is valueless for this purpose.

*Don't let a stranger bluff you; keep asking questions.

*Don't accept a suspicious check simply because it's perforated "insured." This does not mean you are insured.

Danger Signals that often indicate bad checks:

1. Misspellings, particularly of the maker's name.
2. Omission of the maker's name.
3. Unusually high serial numbers (five or more digits).
4. Payroll checks without a cents amount. Remember, 99 times out of 100 payroll checks end in cents.

Precautions to Foil "Skippers"

"Skippers" present another problem. A modicum of protection against these deadbeats can be gained by taking these precautions:

1. Be sure that complete and legible registrations are obtained.
2. Require payment in advance, if you have reason to be suspicious, particularly if the guest is without baggage or checks in late.
3. Some hotels make a person-to-person telephone call to the registered guest at the address he gives. If the guest is bona fide, the call will cost nothing.
4. Limit the amount of the bill you allow guests to run up, setting an appropriate dollar limit on a three-day stay.

The Importance of Security

It has been said that "security is probably the most underestimated responsibility that an innkeeper has." One expert estimates that at least $10 billion is lost annually by American business due to theft, that 30 percent of all business failures each year are the result of employee dishonesty and that seven percent of all bankruptcies in the country are due to pilferage. "Trusted employees," he declares, "outsteal the shoplifter by 15 to 1."

Effective hotel security must concern itself with preventing theft and pilferage, avoiding malicious waste on the part of employees, and the development of emergency plans for the protection of guests in the event of civil disturbances. Prevention, obviously, takes precedence over apprehension.

What To Do to Prevent Robbery

Big city police departments suggest these tips to prevent financial loss or physical injury to employees as a result of attempted robberies:

1. Keep an eye open for suspicious persons loitering on the premises.
2. Maintain a record and description of all valuable property—serial numbers of big bills, identification of cash register and other office equipment, serial numbers of TV sets, etc.
3. When large amounts of cash are sent to the bank, the route taken should be varied from time to time and the trip should be made at different times of the day.
4. Never allow the safe to be open in the presence of strangers.
5. Don't keep too much cash in the register. Use the safe for large amounts of money and get surplus cash to the bank as often as convenient.
6. Install an alarm—electronic beam or other non-obvious type—which can be tripped unobtrusively by the cashier or clerk in the event of a robbery attempt. The best burglary alarm system is the silent central station type which does not warn the thief as does a local alarm such as a siren or bell. In large cities, central alarm systems may be rented from private firms; in small towns they are often tied directly into police headquarters. Frequently part of the cost of installing a silent alarm system will be absorbed by a reduction in burglary insurance premium.
7. Keep all areas of the property—particularly where money is kept—well lighted.
8. Have the number of the local police department right at the front desk telephone so it is handy when needed.
9. Keep a little "bait money" in the safe and cash register. This is money from which the serial numbers have been copied, "marked money" which will make good evidence if found on a suspect.
10. Use closed circuit television to monitor areas such as parking lots and supply rooms where robberies are most likely to occur but which are not under constant direct observation.

New Developments in Security Systems

A number of innovative approaches to improving hotel/motel security are being developed these days.

The Carolando Motor Inn, a 960-room property near Disney World in Orlando, has a security system which substitutes a wallet-sized plastic card for the traditional metal room key.

When a guest registers at the Carolando, a special machine codes several cards at random. One card, the "control card" is inserted in a master console, while one or more cards are given to the guest. When he wishes to unlock the door to his room, the guest inserts the card into a slot near his door. The card he inserts is electronically compared with the corresponding card in the slot matching his room number. If the codes match, the door opens with a click. It is said that it is virtually impossible to inadvertently duplicate a code. In the case of lost or stolen cards, what amounts to an instantaneous change of locksets can be accomplished simply by coding a new set of cards.

Another system utilizes a keyboard to change key and lock combinations by remote control. The keyboard is wired to every lock in the hotel or motel. When a guest registers, his key is "validated" by the keyboard, in effect changing, in less than a second, the key and lock used by the previous occupant of the room.

Guard Against Dishonest Employees

Internal controls can be very effective in limiting thefts or embezzlement by employees. The Fireman's Fund American Insurance Companies suggest these "do's and don'ts":

1. DO KEEP IMPORTANT JOB FUNCTIONS SEPARATED. Don't let the same person make up invoices, bank deposits, check payments and reconcile bank statements.
   Purchasing should also be separated from receiving responsibilities.
2. DO MAKE FREQUENT, SURPRISE SPOT CHECKS. Accounts receivable, inventory, accounts payable, sales and advertising departments should all be subject to examination without warning, as should every other department where cash transactions or valuable goods may be handled.
3. DO ESTABLISH PRINTED CONTROLS ON FORMS. Invoices should be numbered serially at the printer's.
   Delivery tickets should also be prenumbered, and duplicate copies of all forms should be sent to the accounting department for sales and inventory records.
   Checks should be printed on "safety" paper that will not erase.
4. DO ESTABLISH PERSONNEL CONTROLS. Check the job references of prospective employees for the past 10 years.
   If the staff is adequate, rotate employees between jobs.
   Require passes for after-hours entry to certain areas, and check excessive overtime claims.

Without being excessively negative or harmful to morale, let all employees know dishonesty will be prosecuted to the full extent of the law.

5. DON'T LET CUSTOMERS' UNPAID BALANCES ACCUMULATE. To prevent embezzlement of incoming payments, regular notices with return postage paid should be sent to customers with consistent unpaid balances. These can be worded not to offend the customer, and they should be returned to some one other than the person who ordinarily receives payments.

6. DON'T LET AUDITS BE ROUTINE. If an audit is only perfunctory, or if audits are held on regular and unvarying schedules, the embezzler can plan around it, kiting funds to cover lower bank balances or juggling records to hide inventory losses.

7. DON'T IGNORE LARGE BALANCES DUE YOUR SUPPLIERS. Bills you have paid that still show as due are suspect. Payments from you may be siphoned off in your paymaster's office or in the supplier's accounts receivable department.

8. DON'T ECONOMIZE ON LOSS PREVENTION. Use a reputable CPA firm for an extensive audit, preferably at least annually.

    Consult with layout experts and security architects about protective measures for inventory, equipment and important records.

    Ask your insurance company's loss prevention engineers for assistance in developing an overall program to prevent theft.

    And make certain you have enough insurance to cover your potential for loss.

How to Build Hotel and Motel Business with Sound Public Relations and Publicity

Probably no single skill is more vital for success as an innkeeper than public relations ability. Being well and favorably known in the community, on the national scene and to other innkeepers can bring many thousands of dollars worth of business to a property each year. Top hotel managers often develop a following which accompanies them whenever they change jobs. And some prominent hotelmen in years past have become very wealthy through investment tips given to them by favored guests.

What Public Relations Is Not

Public relations is not merely publicity, puffery or "apple polishing." It is *not* manipulation, it is *not* deception, it is *not* the creation of an image unrelated to reality.

Implementing Practical Public Relations

Public relations has been described as "the planned effort to influence opinion through socially responsible performance based on mutually satisfactory two-way communication."

Public relations is being a good neighbor, a good citizen, as well as a good business executive. Ninety percent of public relations is simply the knack of establishing and maintaining good relationships—the other 10 percent is being recognized for your activities and contributions.

These are examples of public relations:

- Public relations is smiling at people;
- Public relations is shoveling snow off the front sidewalk;
- Public relations is having a staff of neat and courteous employees;
- Public relations is having an attractive awning over the front of the establishment on sunny afternoons;
- Public relations is saving an old display item for that freckle-face kid down the street;
- Public relations is asking a father how his children are;
- Public relations is being interested in community activities and taking a dynamic part in local, state and national associations;
- Public relations is remembering a man's name when he comes into your establishment after not having been there for some time;
- Public relations is stopping to talk with a customer;
- Public relations is being an active church or temple member and a civic leader;
- Public relations is keeping your place of business attractive;
- Public relations is lending your support to a Boy Scout or other worthwhile community campaign.

How To Get Publicity

Breaking into the news columns is a lot easier than you may think. If you are elected as an officer of a local club, attend a trade association meeting or sales seminar, make a talk, plan an unusual display or event, your local newspaper will be interested. Send your story typed, double spaced, on one side of the page to the City Editor. In the upper left hand corner, put your name, address and phone number. Unless, for some reason, you don't want to have the story printed right away, put below this: "Release on Receipt." Otherwise, write "Hold for Release (date)." In the "lead"—the first sentence or two—tell the most important facts. Follow this with more complete details.

If you send photographs, they should be 8 X 10 inch glossy black and white pictures with good contrast. The caption, identifying people in the photo "from left to right," should be pasted on the back or at the bottom of the photo. *Never* write on the back of a photo! Be sure to put a piece of cardboard in the envelope with the photo to keep it from being cracked in the mail.

A news release should confine itself to the facts: what happened, when, where, how, why and who was involved. The writer's viewpoint should not be stated, either explicitly or implicitly. It is, of course, quite all right to quote a spokesman's views or analysis of the happening or situation.

A feature story, on the other hand, permits considerably more leeway. Here the object is to dramatize and to provide human interest appeal by colorful description of an event or person from the viewpoint of the writer.

You don't have to be a journalist to get press coverage. If you have the ability to write, or have someone on your staff to prepare press releases, fine. If not, a call to the city desk in which you tell the editor what happened, or what is going to happen, will more often than not bring a reporter to the scene, perhaps a photographer as well, depending on the events. If you are for or against something controversial—such as a local room tax—dropping in to see the paper's editorial writer might pay off in an editorial supporting your position.

Some Good Advice

There are certain "rules of the road" insofar as press relations are concerned. AH&MA Public Relations Director, Al Kudrle offers these suggestions:

DO keep in touch frequently with representatives of all news media—daily and weekly newspaper editors, radio and TV news editors.

DO contact these people only when you have solid factual news such as plans for improvement or a rehabilitation program, appointment of key personnel, open house or career day program for high school students, and the like (always give date, time, place).

DO be fair: Supply same information to all news media at the same time.

DO make sure names are spelled correctly and that the news release is accurate in every respect.

DON'T call the editor to ask if he plans to use the material.

DON'T ask to see a copy of the story before it's printed.

DON'T ask for a tear sheet containing the article. Buy a copy of the paper yourself.

An Important Distinction

It is well to keep in mind at all times that publicity is quite different from advertising. Publicity is not "free" advertising. Propriety and publishing policy are just about the only constraints on an advertising message. But a publicity story must stand on its own as a newsworthy contribution free from hyperbole and hard sell.

PR Is a Two-Way Street

Just as important as initiating press releases is cooperating with the news media when they seek information. Nothing can chill press relations more quickly and completely than the unavailability or silence of a responsible spokesman when the press needs information or an interpretation of a news development, particularly if it is an unfavorable one.

An invaluable aid to insure accuracy in the media whenever they have occasion to refer to your hotel or motel is the development of a press fact sheet. This need not be as elaborate as a convention sales brochure, but can be a simple mimeographed sheet giving the essential data about the property such as:

date and type of construction
assessed valuation
number of rooms
names and home phones of top management
ownership
room rates
significant events in the history of the property
number of employees
total payroll in dollars
local taxes paid
any information of value in writing a feature story
    about the hotel/motel. If "George Washington slept
    here," put it in the fact sheet.

Sources of News and Feature Stories

At the hub of the community, operating generally 24 hours a day, 365 days a year, the hotel/motel should be an inexhaustible source of news and feature stories. Here are some typical possibilities:

- Prominent or unusual guests
- Important meetings
- Significant speeches
- Social events—balls, weddings, charity lunches, etc.
- Community activities, exotic hobbies or praiseworthy achievements of employees
- The physical requirements and consumption of the property—yards of carpet in rooms, numbers of light bulbs, sheets, towels, etc., used weekly.
- Heroic acts of employees or special help given to handicapped guests.
- Community groups using facilities—meeting rooms, swimming pool—provided to them without charge.

Don't Overlook Radio and TV Opportunities

While, in the nature of things, publicity suggests newspapers to most people, radio, TV and other media should not be overlooked.

Keep in contact with your local radio news departments and program directors. "Talk" shows provide good vehicles for interviews with key staff members such as your chef. You might even want to arrange for such a talk show—"Breakfast at _____"—to originate in your hotel/motel with prominent guests participating as interviewees if they are agreeable.

TV also offers good publicity opportunities. Here you should be on the look-out for material with visual impact—how to carve a turkey or prepare an exotic dish demonstrations, speaking appearances by well-known people, athletic tournaments if yours is a resort property.

Local clubs such as Kiwanis and Rotary, and other civic and social organizations should be contacted to offer the services of an appropriate member of the hotel/motel staff as a guest speaker. Suggested talks on a number of interesting innkeeping-related subjects are available from the American Hotel & Motel Association.

Guidelines for Staging a Press Conference

There may come a time when you will decide to hold a press conference. Here are some useful suggestions which will help avoid problems.

1. In general, the best time to hold a press conference is 10 A.M. on a Tuesday, Wednesday, or Thursday. Newspaper deadlines, however, vary from city to city so it is wise to get the advice of the city editor of your local paper or papers on the best time and day. If there are both morning and evening papers, you should try to see that each gets its share of news "breaks."
2. Invitations to the press conference should be sent out about a week ahead of time. They should cover who, where, when, what and why as well as mention of any photo opportunities.
3. Three days before the event, a second copy of the invitation should be sent.
4. The day before the press conference, personal phone calls should be made to all invitees.
5. Make sure the room you select for the conference is large enough for the expected attendance, that the acoustics are good, that it is well ventilated and heated or air conditioned as appropriate, that a PA system in good working order is on hand if the group will be large and that adequate current is available for TV floodlights and other electrical equipment.
6. Tell radio and TV newsmen, when they arrive, where to set up equipment. Arrange special areas where each can interview principals in the press conference afterwards.
7. Keep the conference short and to the point.

   a. Hand out news releases and scripts as invitees come in.
   b. Introduce principals.
   c. Make presentation following format of news release or script.
   d. Question and answer period.
   e. Thank invitees for coming.
8. If some media fail to attend the press conference, arrange for hand delivery of the news release.

Handling an Opening

Different than a press conference is the preview of the opening of a new or expanded facility. Ordinarily, to get the "bugs" out of the operation, a property will first have a "soft" or unpublicized opening at which time it will accept "walk-ins" and some VIP guests. The official opening can be the occasion for considerable ceremony and hoopla. In order to put your best foot forward at this time, observance of these three rules is advised:

1. Do not invite the general public. Invite only the press, local hoteliers, civic leaders and representatives of companies and organizations that may be potential sources of business.
2. Keep the guest list small enough so facilities will not be overtaxed.
3. Check to be sure all facilities and services are in good order. Rehearse ceremonies, reception, service of food and beverages, etc..

Depending on how many guests can be comfortably handled, you might want to consider inviting to the official opening or a follow-up gathering representatives of some or all of the following local businesses or organizations who could be sources of referral business:

1. Airlines
2. Auto rental agencies
3. Realtors
4. Restaurant owners
5. Service station operators
6. Tourist attraction managers
7. Clergymen
8. Neighboring military installations
9. Colleges and private schools

Some Effective Hotel/Motel Public Relations Programs

Several years ago, the American Hotel & Motel Association initiated a Public Relations Achievement Competition for member properties. Winning entries in the annual contest provide dramatic examples of how well-conceived and effectively carried out public relations activities can help promote business, build employee morale and productivity and generate good will in the community.

. . .A Birthday Celebration with a Twist

Ordinarily, the second birthday of a hotel is no big thing. So the Marriott in Bloomington, Minnesota, decided to "celebrate" by putting on an all-day party for 60 retarded children from local schools. When a snow storm hit the city on the eve of the celebration, an inspiration also hit management: stage a snowman building contest for the children. Together with producing members of the Minnesota Vikings football team for autographs and arranging an appearance of Winnie the Pooh and friends, the program resulted in extensive news media coverage as well as 60 ecstatically happy youngsters.

. . .Unifying the Community

A community relations coup was staged by the Ambassador Hotel in Los Angeles which put on a program to unify residents and corporate citizens of the Wilshire area of the city and to call attention to its attractions. Building on the fact that the community had grown around the Ambassador, management invited the entire community to join in a "Walking on Wilshire" parade ending up at the hotel where a picnic lunch and entertainment were provided on the hotel's lawn. Participation by more than 5,000 persons and extensive coverage by news media persuaded Ambassador management and the Wilshire Chamber of Commerce to make the affair an annual event.

. . .Nation-wide TV Coverage at Trifling Cost

The problem of how a medium-size resort motel could create an image and compete successfully with larger and more modern resorts in the Sarasota, Florida, area was solved at trifling cost by the Sheraton Sandcastle. For the price of 50 inexpensive plaques, a single small advertisement and a few dozen sand buckets, the solution—sponsorship of an annual International Sand Castle Building Contest—resulted in reams of publicity and coverage on a nation-wide TV network.

. . .Celebrity Tennis Makes Headlines

When the Washington Hilton opened a new private swimming and tennis club, it sought to attract the attention of official and social Washington in a dramatic way. A Congressional tennis match, with the proceeds going to the favorite charity of the winners, pitted Sen. Pell of Rhode Island and Rep. Symington of Missouri against Sen. Javits of New York and Rep. McClory of Illinois. Gen. William Westmoreland, then Army Chief-of-Staff, refereed. Picture, news, feature, and radio-TV coverage were extensive.

. . .Cherchez les Femmes

Cultivating local secretaries paid off for the management of the Hotel Sonesta in Hartford, Conn.. To encourage the secretaries to book accommodations, meetings and food and beverage functions in the hotel, a monthly newsletter was mailed to some 450 area secretaries. The newsletter reported on activities in the hotel and gave information about its various departments and key management personnel. Monthly drawings were held, using reservation forms mailed with the newsletter as entries, for "week-ends for two" at the hotel. Parties were given for the secretaries by the hotel at Christmas and again in June. As a result, according to the hotel's manager, nearly 90 percent of all its local reservations and repeat business are booked by the secretaries on the hotel's mailing list.

. . .Help for Visitors from Abroad

Helping visitors from abroad cope with the language problem has earned recognition for the giant Travelodge International chain as well as the 64-room Howard Johnson's Motor Lodge in Santa Maria, California. Travelodge, several years ago, established a multi-lingual national toll-free Visit U.S.A. Travel Information Telephone Center in cooperation with the U. S. Travel Service and without cost to the government. The program, still operating, provides impartial answers in appropriate languages to foreign visitors on attractions, public transportation, accommodations and other travel topics. Users of the service need simply dial one toll-free number from anywhere in the country.

In Santa Maria, the manager of the Howard Johnson's Motor Lodge organized an interpreter service for visitors from abroad to the city. Utilizing the volunteer services of local junior college students who spoke a foreign language fluently, the program provided visitors from abroad with answers by telephone to questions about attractions, dining, accommodations and information about the community.

. . . Boosting Employee Morale

The Cosmopolitan Hotel in Denver, Colorado, won an award for a public relations campaign aimed at overcoming a letdown in employee morale arising from a change in ownership of the hotel. Among the elements of the program to improve employee communication, morale and productivity were these:

1. An employee council was set up to facilitate upward communication and to increase employee involvement.
2. A monthly employee publication was originated.
3. An improved employee orientation program was initiated.
4. A program was set in motion to honor an Employee-of-the-Month for unusual loyalty or dedication to his job.

. . .Calling P.T. Barnum

Ground-breaking and the official opening of a new hotel or motel present endless possibilities for public relations-publicity gambits. International chains such as Inter-Continental Hotels mark these events with panoplies of food, libations and celebrities rivaling affairs of state.

Here in the U.S., Marriott Hotels has taken the lead when it comes to imaginative—even daring—staging of ground-breaking and opening programs.

Typical of the Marriott approach was the ground-breaking of the 956-room New Orleans Marriott which saw some 250 celebrities marching behind Pete Fountain and the Onward Brass Band through the French Quarter to the site. On signal, a giant balloon materialized and rose to the exact height the new hotel was to reach when completed. Clustered around it were hundreds of smaller "satellite" balloons.

At the opening, a beauty queen dove from five stories up cutting a ribbon on her descent to an air cushion at ground level. Twenty-four "Miss Marriotts," representing sister properties, were on hand for the festivities. The honor of cutting loose a giant balloon with the symbolic key to the hotel's front entrance attached went to "Miss New Orleans Marriott."

Culminating at the opening ceremony was a National Antique Auto Race with one notable entry, the "Marriott Charriott," gathering greetings from mayors of cities on its route to New Orleans.

A PR Activity for the Whole Industry

Perhaps the most concise explanation of public relations is that it consists of "doing good and getting credit for it." By this measure, one of the most rewarding public relations activities an innkeeper can engage in at the present time is support of efforts to preserve a quality environment in and around his property as well as in his community. To guide the nation's innkeepers in this mutually beneficial activity, the AH&MA's Committee for a Quality Environment has developed the following pledge:

Innkeeper's Pledge to Maintain Quality Environment

"As an innkeeper, my success depends on a clean environment as well as on service and a quality product. Not only do I depend on the environment for today's business, but I recognize the importance of maintaining a quality environment to permit future growth. I am aware that man depends on nature, and that man must work with, not against, nature.

"Whenever I plan new facilities, I must acknowledge my responsbility to give approval and direction to architects and building contractors that will minimize contributions to pollution and visual blight. This is an obligation to my neighbors as well as to future progress.

"Therefore, with full recognition that these requirements might increase project costs, I agree to accept all seven points of the following pledge:

"1. My construction plans will specify that as many trees and shrubs or as much ground cover, will remain untouched, as possible. Should trees have to be removed, healthy new trees will be planted in other areas of the site.

"2. Attractive landscaping will be planned.

"3. The contractor will be required to schedule his work so that as little raw earth as possible will be exposed to the elements for the shortest possible time. If the construction site is large, or the schedule prolonged, to minimize erosion, vegetation or mulch will be placed on the raw earth, and sediment basins will be built to keep neighboring ravines, streams, rivers and lakes free from silt pollution.

"4. At all times, the contractor will be encouraged to keep the building site neat and clean. This decreases visual blight as well as minimizes windblown trash that might degrade neighboring property.

"5. There will be no trash burned at the site. In this way the project will not contribute to air pollution. Also, whenever possible, the contractor will be asked not to burn trees or timber.

"6. When poisonous chemicals must be used for termite control, to avoid polluting the soil, application will be directed by a qualified, bonded expert.

"7. The least possible amount of ground will be paved to minimize water runoff that causes erosion and kills plants, trees and grass. When a large area of pavement is required for functional reasons, trees and/or plant beds will be built into the area."

Strategic Planning for Exceptional Hotel/Motel Profits

Whether planning a new facility or improving an operating property, the astute manager needs to make a careful analysis of a great many factors.

Probably the most crucial consideration of all is location. Ellsworth M. Statler, one of the greatest innovators the lodging industry has known, is said to have responded, when asked the three most important factors in the success of a hotel: "Location, location, and location." While this view is undoubtedly an over-simplification, there is little question but that *where* a hotel or motel is located can be a major determinant of its occupancy and profits.

The location of commercial lodging facilities mirrors the travel and traffic patterns of the times. Among the earliest inns were those established at oases on oriental trading routes. Later, reflecting the popular modes of transportation of the day, concentrations of hotels or motels were erected at quayside, along post roads, at interstate interchanges and, more recently, near airports.

During the past few years many motor inns have been built near special facilities such as hospitals, colleges, industrial parks and attractions such as Disney World in Florida.

Significantly, the extension of the Interstate Highway system has restricted rather than encouraged construction of motels along highways. Among the reasons for this are the longer distances that can be driven in a day, the greater speeds at which it is possible to travel, and the limited number of exits that are available.

Criteria for Choosing a Good Location

Ideally, a feasibility study should be the first order of business in planning a hotel or motel. But there are a number of site-related items that can be checked beforehand by visual inspection and a little judicious quizzing of "friendly natives."

1. *Visibility*—Can the site be seen clearly from all approaches and at today's fast driving speeds?
2. *Traffic*—A count of total traffic past the site can be deceptive. "Locals" may provide some restaurant and bar business, but the transients are the ones who account for room sales.
3. *Access*—Is it easy to get to the site from the highway, or do road dividers, one-way streets, traffic lights, etc., pose a problem for the would-be guest?
4. *Intercepting Position*—Is the property located at a point where travelers would be likely to slow down or stop—at a major intersection, throughway exit, or at a point where travel services are available?
5. *Surroundings*—Is the site near travel objectives such as a convention center, tourist attractions, community services such as drugstores, drive-in restaurants and theaters, coin-operated laundry, service stations, variety stores, shopping centers, etc.?
6. *Proximity of Competition*—Contrary to what many believe, there are advantages in locating a hotel or motel near others: people tend to "shop" motel areas; there can be referrals from other properties when they are full; a lodging complex provides the capability of handling conventions or other large groups.
7. *Absence of Nuisance*—Since a good night's rest is what the traveler is looking for, it is important that the motel not be down wind or nearby a railroad, noisy manufacturing operations, slaughter houses, chemical plants, etc.
8. *Topography*—A good motel site should be rectangular in shape and provide ample space for parking and room for expansion. It should allow for construction of the motel well back from the highway. To be avoided are rights of way, odd-shaped plots, ledge rock or wet soil.
9. *Cost of land*—As a rule of thumb, not more than 20 percent of the total cost of the project should go into land acquisition and site development.

Site location help can be obtained from qualified landscape architects. A list may be obtained from the American Society of Landscape Architects, 2000 K Street N.W., Washington, D. C. 20006. Chain operations such as Holiday Inns, Ramada Inns and others provide site selection assistance to prospective franchisees.

Feasibility Study Is a "Must"

The most rewarding investment a prospective hotel/motel owner can make at the outset is arranging for a feasibility study to be made by a competent professional organization. A study of this kind will do three things:

1. Determine if there is a market for a new hotel or motel and what kind of market it is;
2. Recommend a site appropriate to this market; and
3. Project income and expenses of the proposed property.

The first step in the feasibility study is to gather all pertinent information about the community to determine if it can support a new hotel or motel and what kind of property would have the best chance of success. A great many factors need to be considered such as location in respect to other cities in the area; mileages to major cities, resorts, etc.; community population and population trends; transportation; and an economic profile including consideration of industries, colleges, military installations, special events such as fairs, retail trading area and sales trends, bank deposits, etc.. *A general rule is that a community will support two first-class rooms per thousand population.*

A detailed study should be made of other hotels and motels in the area to determine their occupancy, rate range, number of rooms, type and quality of accommodations provided, whether there are adequate facilities in existence for banquet and group functions and the existence of sites for potential competitors in the future.

Consideration needs also to be given to the number, types, and prosperity of local businesses, local employment, type of residential areas, number of conventions and business or trade meetings that the community might attract, and natural or man-made attractions which would appeal to tourists.

With land values soaring, and the cost of building and furnishing a hotel or motel at well over $20,000 a room generally, there is too much at stake to allow snap judgments or an amateur approach to determining the economic feasibility of a contemplated lodging facility investment. This is best left to the professionals, firms such as Harris, Kerr, Forster or Laventhol, Krekstein, Horwath & Horwath, which have considerable expertise in these matters.

Purpose Influences Location

Obviously, there is no one all-purpose location for a hotel/motel. Those considerations which would be vital for a highway motel are not necessarily applicable to a downtown motor hotel. And a resort property would have many site requirements different from the first two.

Then, too, consideration needs to be given to the kind of guests the property is expected to attract. Although they need not be mutually exclusive, categories of transient guests which might influence location, design, etc., include business travelers, vacationers, and people attending conventions, sporting events or other local attractions. Finally, the hotel/motel might be planned as a "destination" where guests would simply relax, enjoy the scenery, climate or sports facilities. As a general rule, properties that are connected with a franchise or referral chain do well almost irrespective of location because of the business generated by national advertising and referrals within the chain.

Looking ahead, the hotel/motel planner needs to be aware of changing travel patterns and preferences such as movement of industry to the suburbs and rural areas, the surge in popularity of camper travel, and development of STOL and VTOL aircraft.

The Importance of Integration

The pages of innkeeping history are replete with examples of poor planning, design and construction. In the Caribbean area, one large hotel had to build a second pool when it found that the original one was shaded all day by the hotel itself. There have been cases where hotels have been built with only a few hundred guest rooms to accompany convention facilities for more than a thousand, and without the ability to expand. *In a large hotel in Pennsylvania with function space for several thousand on a single floor, no guest toilet facilities are available on that floor. Perhaps the worst gaffe occurred many years ago when it was discovered, only a few days before a new hotel was to open, that the architect had failed to provide for a kitchen!*

In a word, the trend today in hotel/motel planning, design and construction is "integration." Aware that travelers seek an "experience" over mere convenience and comfort, architects and designers try to create an ambience that begins with the exterior, is maintained in the lobby and public areas, continues in the guest rooms and usually reaches its peak in the specialty restaurants and/or night clubs. A phenomenally successful example of this concept is the Regency Hotel in Atlanta where the design creates a contemporary, "alive" atmosphere which sets the scene for the hotel's facilities and services.

Modular Construction Saves Time, Cuts Costs

Certainly the most promising recent development in hotel/motel building is modular construction. By cutting construction time and costs by as much as 40 percent as compared to traditional construction methods, this technique may be the answer to the drastic increase in building costs in recent years which has seen hotel construction costs alone in some areas pass $30,000 per room. Motel construction costs per unit range from around $8,000 to the neighborhood of $20,000 where a considerable amount of space for restaurants and function rooms is included.

In modular construction, room units are constructed separately and hoisted into place by crane. The usual procedure is to place in forms all necessary electrical and plumbing conduits, along with reinforcing steel, and to pour concrete to form the room module. After curing, the unit is ready to be trucked to the site and placed into position. Apart from relatively low cost and time saved in construction, modular buildings are obviously fire-resistant and virtually soundproof.

"Slip Forming" Cuts Months from Construction Time

Another new wrinkle in hotel/motel construction which has appeared recently is the "slip forming" technique of concrete extrusion. Used to raise the exterior walls and some of the interior structure of a 15-story hotel in St. Petersburg, Florida, it enabled the property to be "topped out" in just eight days.

In Norfolk, Virginia, the slip forming technique used in constructing a 14-story motor inn enabled the builders to cut three months from the normal construction time for a property of this size. In the Norfolk property a three-foot thick reinforced slab was poured for the foundation. Then, using a specially constructed wood and steel form, workmen poured concrete into the form continuously at the average rate of 9½ inches per hour. At the same time the form was raised by a number of electrically operated hydraulic jacks while steel reinforcing rods were inserted into the concrete.

Figure 13-1

Atlanta's Regency Hyatt House has become a showplace as well as a top ranked hotel. It is noteworthy for architect John Portman's atrium design with its feeling of openness, a massive cocktail lounge ceiling suspended by a single cable from the roof of the structure and glass-walled elevators which seemingly rise by levitation.

The Shape of Things to Come

Along with revolutionary new construction methods, advances are also taking place in the *configuration* of hotels/motels. Travelodge International, which pioneered the tri-arc style, attributes the following advantages to it:

Figure 13-2

Nine story TraveLodge motor hotel in Houston, Texas is typical of chain's TRI-ARC design.

    A. Each room has a view.
    B. The wedge shape of guest rooms permits each to have an unusually large bath and dressing area.
    C. The central core, containing elevators, linen rooms, utilities and ice cube machines, facilitates economies in construction and operation.

Like the tri-arc, besides the plus of distinctive appearance, cylinder-like hotel/motel structures offer the advantages of being able to concentrate service and utility equipment at the center core with resultant lower construction and operating costs, and to have all guest rooms on the outside with views. Additionally, they are ready-made for the popular rooftop revolving restaurants or lounges and they offer minimum resistance to wind. Still other advantages claimed for the circular building are suitability for sites where land costs are high and/or minimum area is available and compatibility with circumferential ramps leading to parking.

"The answer to how to build today for tomorrow is to build structures that are most adaptable to what our guests would like to have. Not what we would like to see, not what our architects feel is necessary, but what the public wants," a leading construction tycoon told hotel/motel leaders.[1]

Experts Critical of Hotel/Motel Design

Designer Henry End says that two-thirds of the hotel rooms in service today are dull and drab, without charm. Architect Thomas F. Hennessy points out that changes in modes of transportation, vacation time and methods of conducting business are creating new needs in facilities.

Ignoring what the public wants or needs can be very costly. A major hotel in the South had to spend nearly $300,000 a few years after it was built to add a swimming pool not originally planned.

Well, then, what *does* the public want? According to Morris Lapidus, noted hotel architect responsible for some of Miami's most glamorous edifices, hotel guests fall into two categories—business travelers and pleasure travelers. Both groups expect something different in a hotel than they'll find at home. The business traveler wants a comfortable bed, easily accessible closet and drawer space, good lighting for reading, excellent lighting for make-up or shaving and unobtrusive fast service.

The leisure traveler appreciates all these niceties, but above all he wants the atmosphere of his hotel and his room to reflect the ambience of the city or country in which he is visiting without detracting from the quality of the service. He wants to feel as though he really is away from home.

Objective: Maximum Occupancy with Minimum Maintenance

Since there appears to be little, if any, demand anymore for the "home away from home" type of accommodation and, as Lapidus states, "Any effort to capture the feeling of home in a hotel room is futile and expensive," today's innkeeper should be guided by what will give him maximum occupancy with minimum maintenance costs.

Emphasis needs to be placed on furnishings designed specifically for hotel and motel use, materials that are attractive yet easy to maintain, suspended desks and chests providing a feeling of spaciousness while cutting cleaning time by half; lamps, TV and other fixtures permanently attached to walls or furniture to prevent their being knocked over or removed.

In deciding on the type and size of rooms a property should have, consideration needs to be given to location and type of guest served. A resort or highway property

---

[1]"How to Build Today for Tomorrow", Wayne B. Duddlesten, President Tex-Craft Builders, Inc., American Hotel & Motel Assoc. Convention, Miami Beach, Florida, December 10, 1965.

should have a relatively high percentage of twin and larger rooms and connecting rooms that can be made into suites to accommodate family groups. The city hotel or motel can do with a higher number of singles although the trend overall is to larger rooms and larger beds. As a matter of fact, two double beds in a room is becoming almost standard and even singles are likely to be furnished with a double bed since it is becoming increasingly common for an individual occupying a room to request a double bed.

The studio-type room, which is designed to serve as bedroom at night and living room or temporary office by day is perhaps better in theory than in practice. As a rule, businessmen do not like the idea of making their own beds at night, particularly if this requires a search for the component parts.

Sheraton's "Copyrighted Room"

Figure 13-3

The unique plan for the bathroom results from human factors considerations: relationships of fixtures; lighting; surface treatments. Controls for showers and tub are accessible from the room proper. The form of the bath produces interesting interior and exterior conformations. Projecting out from the building wall, this bath unit accommodates present construction systems and is adaptable to possible unitized approaches in the future.

Figure 13-4

Twin double beds will be standard for many future Sheraton rooms. One (seen as a sofa) is combined with chest and refectory top, creating a visual and real barrier between living/sleeping areas. By eliminating waste space—principally a corridor—the living segment can represent more than 41% of the gross area.

Figure 13-5

One of several room conformations developed for planned use in new Sheraton hotels and motor inns, the living/sleeping areas are separated by the low bed/chest/sofa divider. Outboard placement of bath provides interesting interior alcove and exterior configuration.

The most revolutionary concept in guest room design in at least 50 years was unveiled a few years ago by Sheraton Corporation. Analyzing space utilization from the guest's viewpoint, it was found that, for the in-room activities of the typical Sheraton guest—entertaining, working and relaxing, as well as sleeping—he needed a suite rather than just a bedroom. Further investigation revealed that, in traditional hotel bedrooms, there was an inordinate amount of wasted circulation space and a correspondingly awkward arrangement of furniture.

As a result of this study, Sheraton came up with a "copyrighted room" the fundamental breakthrough of which is the placement of bathrooms on the *outside* wall rather than along the corridors. This relocation results in a room with considerably more living space and makes possible the installation and easy replacement of prefabricated bathrooms.

A further step—consideration of furniture arrangements to improve space flexibility—led to selection of a new piece of furniture serving as a combination chest of drawers, sofa and full double bed achieved by mounting a conventional bed on an inclined track which can be locked into position as a sofa or extended to serve as a second bed in the room. Given the potential flexibility of this convertible bed, Sheraton reasoned that the first bed could be put on a permanent base eliminating the need for carpeting or cleaning under it. The net effect of relocating the bathroom, angling a wall to open up the view, and taking a new look at furniture design and arrangment was to provide, in essentially the same overall area, more than twice the living space as could be obtained with the traditional layout.

Because of union objections, Sheraton's "Room of Tomorrow" is still on the drawing board.

Hints on Furnishings

While a number of motel chains have been meeting with success in offering Spartan accommodations at low prices, many travelers still seem to want the amenities and are willing to pay for them. The highly regarded Century Plaza Hotel in Los Angeles lists these items as essential to a good room: oversized beds, color television, selective piped-in music, electric blankets and alarm clock, black-out draperies, game table with chairs, built-in refrigerator with ice maker, and (a bow to California weather) a balcony-lanai with furniture.

As for furniture style, the one "no-no" seems to be "clinical modern." In addition to being unattractive to many guests, it is somehow incongruous in luxury type accommodations. Early American, and 18th or 19th century English styling are popular in virtually all price ranges, with luxury establishments favoring French period furniture.

Coming back to the theme of integration, the furnishings of the guest bedrooms, the lobby, front desk, dining rooms, cocktail lounges and meeting rooms should all blend together to create a merchandisable atmosphere. Rather than each reflecting a different period or theme, they should carry out the one such as English tavern, Early American, French Provincial, or Scandinavian Contemporary.

Let There Be Light

Although inadequate lighting is a frequent source of irritation to hotel guests, there is a more positive reason for giving attention to this aspect of decor. Light not only illuminates, it can help create a mood, an atmosphere which makes food more appetizing, bedrooms more restful, public rooms more warm and friendly.

Effective exterior lighting requires illumination of the hotel sign so that it is visible at a distance and stands out from surrounding lighted areas. Both the entrance sign and entrance roadway should be illuminated at a level considerably higher than street or highway lighting—the sign at a level of from three to five times higher and the entrance roadway at least twice as bright. Wherever possible, accent exterior lighting should be used to highlight landscaping and/or the facade of the building. The most satisfactory type of exterior area lighting is provided by color corrected mercury vapor lamps mounted on anodized aluminum poles.

Lobby lighting should extend an invitation to the guest as well as provide adequate illumination for the work performed at the front desk. The higher level of illumination required at the work area is usually best achieved by fluorescent lights while the warmer, more subdued lighting in the rest of the lobby is obtained by the use of incandescent bulbs in attractive fixtures.

Poorly lighted hallways are a false economy since they not only create a dismal atmosphere for guests, but may be an invitation to criminal activities.

The guest room should have an overhead light controlled from the entrance, lighted closets, enough properly located wall outlets so long cords for lamps or TV are not necessary, good reading lights over each chair, lights conveniently placed for reading in bed and at least one light that can be turned on or off without getting out of bed. The bathroom should have, in addition to an overhead light, fluorescent lamps with shields to illuminate the shaving mirror, and, particularly if it has two lavatories, an array of incandescent lights over a second make-up mirror.

Lighting the Restaurant

Although a food operation deals with merchandising a product geared to the sense of taste, much of its success comes from appealing to the customers' sense of sight. Apart from using lighting that keeps food looking appetizing, it is important to have it reflect the kind of operation it serves. For example, a breakfast room or coffee shop at noon should be well lighted not only for a cheery atmosphere, but to stimulate turnover. At dinner time, subdued lighting may encourage lingering, but it also may persuade guests to make an occasion of the meal by ordering more expensive items along with wine and the other niceties of gracious dining.

In addition to the general area lighting of the food service operation, it is desirable to have some kind of extra light at each table whether provided by spots in the ceiling, cove lighting or lamps. For mood and atmosphere, however, lighting should also focus on vertical surfaces—oil paintings, a brick wall, sculpture, grained wood.

To be sure proper and adequate illumination is provided in all areas, it is recommended that the foot-candle suggestions contained in the IES Lighting Handbook published by the Illuminating Engineering Society, 345 East 47 Street, New York, New York, be adhered to.

Ten Ways to Save Money on Lighting

1. Provide *adequate*, but not excessive illumination
2. Select the most appropriate fixtures and illumination level for each purpose.
3. Choose lamps with switches at the base to lessen the chance of accidental breakage. Better yet, wherever possible use wall or hanging units.
4. Be sure all fixtures have the Underwriters' Laboratories seal for fire prevention and longer life.
5. Remember that, in general, fluorescent lights provide more illumination than incandescent bulbs for each unit of power consumed.
6. Replacement of bulbs on a regular schedule based on life expectancy is less costly than only replacing them when necessary. Bulbs on their "last legs" use as much electricity as fresh ones, but provide considerably less light.
7. When buying fixtures, keep the cost of maintenance in mind.
8. Instruct employees to turn off lights when not needed.
9. Remind guests to turn off lights when leaving their rooms.
10. Be sure bulbs and fluorescent tubes are cleaned with a damp cloth occasionally to insure that they are delivering full illumination.

Special Equipment Requirements for Business Meetings

Although business meetings are an important source of revenue for many hotels, relatively few of them provide the equipment and facilities that modern meeting planners require.

The minimum requirement in a typical meeting room, according to the Hotel Sales Management Association, is "the required number of chairs arranged in the form requested, a platform, a presiding officer's table and chairs, a lighted lectern (either table or floor type), a gavel, ice water and glasses on the speaker's table, a blackboard, chalk, eraser and pointer, and an American Flag (which belongs at every public gathering held in the United States)."

But with the wide range of audio-visual tools available and with the increasing sophistication of those who plan and attend meetings, basic meeting room requirements of the Seventies are considerably more demanding. These key points should be considered by both meeting planners and hotel hosts.

1. Entrance and exit facilities for materials and properties, as well as guests, facilitating movement without delay.
2. Adequate parking for guests and meeting sponsor's vans.
3. Safety features including properly marked fire exits, properly fused circuits, adequate floorload capacity and flame-proofed draperies.

Figure 13-6

Luxuriously appointed meeting room for small groups, one of several such facilities at New York Sheraton.

4. Adequate electric circuits, 20 amperes minimum capacity, with outlets at both front and rear of room. It should be possible to control all room lights from a single switch, preferably at the rear of the room where projection equipment would be located. This switch should *not* also turn off projection equipment outlets or the lighted speaker's lectern. Dimmer controls to allow partial illumination for note taking during film projection are a desirable feature.

5. For the comfort and convenience of the audience, air conditioning and heating should be controlled by a room thermostat which can easily be adjusted without the services of the hotel engineer. Ventilation should be provided and washrooms and drinking fountains should be nearby. Chairs should be more comfortable than the folding type often provided.

6. Special room darkening facilities other than venetian blinds and draperies should be provided.

7. Ceiling height should be adequate to accommodate a large screen above the stage. Rooms with low ceilings cause audiences to become restless and usually have poor acoustics.

8. Top-quality sound systems are a must. In addition to the lectern "mike," there should be provision for "lavaliere" microphones for panelists and portable microphones for audience participation.

9. A usual complement of "props" will include easels and blackboards, tables and chairs for panelists and speakers, and an adequate size screen. Authorities recommend that the screen be at least 6' x 8' for rooms less than 40' long, 8' x 10' for 40' rooms and 10' x 12' or larger for big ballrooms.

10. A "must" is house staff available to help in setting up the room and equipment for a meeting.
11. Fast food and beverage service should be provided for "breaks" and meals. Some properties which do a large meeting business such as Chicago's O'Hare Inn, have a separate wing with its own kitchen for meetings.
12. At the rear of the meeting room, there should be a projection table, platform or booth, depending on the size of the room and the lavishness of the facility. Purpose is to provide convenient outlets and space for projection equipment and to keep audience distraction to a minimum.

Installations of a more ambitious kind could—and probably should—include tape and possibly videotape recording and playback equipment, record player, two-way closed circuit television, and rear-screen projection.

Probably the ultimate in meeting or training facilities is the learning center concept which Marriott Hotels has implemented on a national basis. A central core contains just about every kind of audio-visual equipment imaginable and serves several classrooms radiating off it.

Smaller properties that find it uneconomical to own meeting equipment need to arrange with local suppliers for fast and dependable service on rentals. Equipment for which there will be a demand includes: 16 mm sound projector, slide projector, tape recorder, and sound amplification equipment (PA).

How to Cut Telephone Department Losses

Down through the years, the cost of providing guest telephone service has been a sizeable drain on innkeeping industry profits. The American Hotel & Motel Association estimates that the industry's loss on this account is in the order of $55 million yearly. A study in New York State several years ago revealed that the typical hotel in that state loses 12.5¢ on each local call; 4¢ on each interstate call and 8.6¢ on each intrastate call.

Industry efforts, spearheaded by AH&MA, have resulted in favorable adjustment of rates and equipment rental charges in a number of states, and individual properties have been able to achieve substantial savings through careful checking of bills submitted by the telephone company.

A promising new way to save on telephone department expenses appeared on the horizon in 1968 with the Federal Communications Commission ruling, in the Carterfone Case, allowing interconnection of privately-owned telephone equipment to telephone company lines. Unfortunately, privately-owned equipment is no panacea that will guarantee trouble-free service and reduce costs. Careful study of many factors is required before deciding on the installation of private telephone equipment as against a system leased from the telephone company. In addition to the prudent step of getting bids from several suppliers, including the telephone company, consideration needs to be given to costs and problems of installation and repair, reliability and flexibility of equipment, expansion capability and optional features available.

While, in most cases, it may be cheaper to own your own telephone system than to pay monthly bills to the telephone company, this is not always true.

In making a choice between the telephone company and having your own telephone system, a good rule of thumb is this:

If your monthly rates are lower with a private system, and if you will own the equipment outright in less than 10 years, your best bet is to acquire your own system.

In figuring monthly rates, include: interest, installation charges, maintenance costs, insurance, changes in tax position due to acquisition of taxable property.

Also, since service is such an important consideration, be sure that the private system manufacturer (1) has a service center within an hour's drive of your property and (2) will provide emergency call response within two hours.

Check List to Control Telephone Costs

Is each item of equipment used and necessary?

One unnecessary switchboard light can cost as much as $45 a year.

Can you eliminate some trunk lines and extension lines?

Can you make do with less complicated and less expensive equipment?

Can you reduce the number of operators required by using more sophisticated equipment?

Have you asked the telephone company for a detailed itemization of all telephone equipment?

Have you checked to be sure you have everything listed and that it is working?

Many hotels and motels have gotten refunds and credits for equipment not on their premises or charged for more than once.

Are you receiving all toll call commissions to which you are entitled?

Are you taking advantage of deductions many telephone companies allow on charges for toll calls made by guests who leave without paying their bills?

Have you had the telephone company make a traffic study, at no cost to you, to determine switchboard requirements?

Are you taking advantage of suspended service rate if there is a sharp seasonal drop in switchboard use?

Do you ask the telephone company to make free, periodic, trunk busy studies?

You can save as much as $300 annually by having a single infrequently used trunk removed.

Have you considered eliminating extra cost options such as seldom used extensions, private lines, dial intercom, call director?

Do you make it easy for guests to use coin telephones for local calls?

A hotel/motel generally loses money in handling local calls placed from guest rooms. If the calls are placed from a coin telephone, however, they produce a profit for the property.

Do you keep a tight rein on use of hotel/motel telephones for personal calls?

Do you take advantage of savings possible through direct dialing and station calls instead of person-to-person?

Have you investigated possible savings through WATS service (flat rate billing for long distance calls, both incoming and outgoing)?

For high traffic service to a particular city or office, are you using tie lines?

Do you check charges on telephone bills carefully?

One 75-room hotel discovered, under a new accounting set-up, that it had been overbilled for local calls over a long period. A negotiated settlement with the telephone company gave the hotel credit for 5,000 calls.

Managers of small hotels and motels report savings of up to $100 a month as a result of claims submitted to the telephone company for overcharges and "skipper" allowances. Refunds for some larger hotels have exceeded $2,500 a month.

Have you considered hiring a communication consultant?

Small to medium-size hotels and motels report saving thousands of dollars a year on Telephone Department expenses as a result of recommendations made by competent telephone consultants.

Six Ways to Boost Profits

1. *Cater to your guests.* Learn their likes and dislikes and make them feel you are interested. Give an extra bit of service.
2. *Improve your image.* Use the tools of advertising and publicity to build a reputation for quality and service.
3. *Encourage teamwork.* Keep your employees informed and give them a voice in making decisions they will be responsible for implementing. Teach them what to do, how to do it and when to do it. Then *let* them do it.
4. *Plan ahead.* Estimate your sales and cash flow for the next five years. Start now to make plans for financial growth.
5. *Look for profit volume.* Keep expenses in line. Use your break-even point as a control. Beware of the tendency to assume that big sales volume is necessarily equated with high profit volume. Profit is what is left after the bills have been paid.
6. *Pay your civic rent.* Your hotel or motel's growth and prosperity are closely related to the growth and character of your community. Take an active interest in the organizations that work to build a good community.

"There is nothing which has yet been contrived by man, by which so much happiness is produced as by a good inn."

Dr. Samuel Johnson

INDEX